D1649088

BOOTLEGGER'S SON

One man's journey from his
earthly father to his heavenly father

By E.G. "Leo" Koury

With Dennis Seeds
and contributions from John Ettorre

To Bruce,
My FAVORITE Cousins!
GOD BLESS!
Cousin Leo

Bootlegger's Son
COPYRIGHT © 2016 E.G. Koury

Published by:
Smart Business Network
835 Sharon Drive, Suite 200
Westlake, OH 44145

Printed in the United States of America
Editor: Dustin S. Klein
Cover and Interior design: Jim Mericsko

ISBN: 978-0-9839983-2-7
Library of Congress Control Number: 2016936067

DEDICATION

Thank you, God, for blessing me with a wonderful, spiritual wife, Lila, who has been patient, forgiving and supportive of me during our 57 years of marriage (and counting).

Thank you, God, for bringing us four wonderful, God-fearing children—Lisa, Fred, Janet and Lee; as well as their wonderful spiritual spouses—Jimmy, Lena, Tony and Gretchen. And a special thank-you to Fred for his encouragement to write this book, which also I want to dedicate to the memory of my father, Fred Koury.

I also appreciate our nine grandchildren—Richard, Jennifer, Stefanie, Eli, Halle, Annie, Lila, Michael and Joey. May God grant them many years of health, wisdom and spirituality.

I humbly submit that my coming to Christ was because He died on the cross for my sins and gave me salvation. Over the years, I came to realize the success I attained in my profession came from Him, guiding me each step of the way. It is because of Him that I was able to surround myself with bright people who made all the wonderful contributions that led to success and achievements that made me appear to be very smart. Back then, my ego was big. But it was through Him that I learned about humility and how to approach life by being more humble—something I wasn't able to do in my pre-Christian way of life and still struggle with daily.

Beyond my family and God, I've always been fond of Vince Lombardi, the famous coach of the Green Bay Packers, who said, "The difference between a successful person and others is not the lack of strength, not a lack of knowledge, but rather a lack of will."

Finally, I would like to thank God for His unconditional love and grace. It is through my relationship with Him that I've come to have greater understanding and appreciation for my earthly father.

Your humble servant,
Leo

FOREWORD

*"And he shall turn the heart of the fathers to the children
and the heart of the children to the fathers."*
—Malachi 4:6

After he experienced God's amazing grace at a 1994 Billy Graham Crusade, Leo Koury turned his heart to his heavenly Father—and for the first time had a change of heart about his verbally abusive earthly father, whose young life was embittered by World War I era Lebanon. Leo then realized his father had been there for him all the time and loved him.

There would be many memories, experiences, challenges, hardships and victories—filled with tears and laughter, but ultimately this is a story about a son and a father, and how God shed a light on Leo to see a much bigger picture.

Without him having a relationship with God, Leo would have been bankrupt of a father's love. Life would just have passed him by. He never would have seen his father accurately or the people who came in to his life to make a difference.

Leo came to see his father for the man he truly was—kind, caring, loyal and sacrificial—who always sought the best for his children and wanted them to succeed in America. But Leo's father, Fred Koury, could not express the love his son so desperately wanted to feel. Leo didn't realize that since his father lacked opportunity and didn't make the best choices, it made him want to live his life through Leo. Fred Koury's life meant sacrificing his name and being the patriarch for his family—five households—and dying at a young age from the burden. Leo's father saw the success, power and prestige lawyers held in society and directed him into higher education and the legal field.

A pivotal step in Leo's change of heart was to see his father's homeland. He completed a full circle, realizing where his dad had come from, what the situation was under the Ottoman Empire and all the hardships people who lived there faced. And then it dawned on him: The son has returned to the homeland country and the reconciliation has begun.

But the story does not end there. Today Leo recognizes it is by God's grace that he has a strong relationship with his own children, grandchildren and the many people he has influenced.

And recently with a group of those cherished ones, Leo completed a parallel circle, visiting the Billy Graham Library and renewing his relationship with the teachings of Billy Graham 20 years after the Crusade in Cleveland, Ohio, where he accepted Christ.

When Leo was able to see his father through a different lens and with a personal relationship with God, he saw that his father really did love him. May you be inspired by Leo's story to find the peace and contentment available to you.

— John Murtha, December 2015
Former director of WEC USA
WEC is an international mission organization
with ministries in more than 60 countries

AUTHOR'S NOTE

I t took 20 years to write this book. The story—although filled with numerous anecdotes or my adventures—never really came together in a meaningful way until recently.

Before that, I thought this book would be about me and my life, and in some small way serve as a way to honor my father's memory. But as it was written, the goal became much more meaningful. Not only does this story reflect upon the life I've lived so far and honor my father for all the things he did for me, it also provided clarity about my father's intentions and his deep-seeded love for me. It's something not a lot of sons have the opportunity to do, and for that I'm grateful.

Growing up, my father's discipline and rough ways were so archaic and foreign that they were difficult to comprehend. I didn't realize at the time that he was giving me a gift from his experience, telling me in his own way what life was really about.

The book also stalled because I hadn't taken the time to sit down and reflect upon my relationship with God. When I came to Christ in the 1990s, my outlook on life became that much clearer; however, the relationships all around me that guided my life's path weren't evident. These people were all around me, shaping who I was and who I am today. But I was simply too close to see the big picture of what was happening. Plus, there was a serious chip on my shoulder that came from being known as a bootlegger's son. That was something that took too many years to embrace—transforming its meaning from one of a badge of shame to that of a badge of honor. Only then, did the pieces that make up this book coalesce to become the story you read here.

My father, Fred Koury, emigrated from Lebanon in the early 1920s when he was about 18 years of age. He fled to escape the cruel Ottoman Empire rule over Lebanon. With its tyranny and the lack of opportunity during the occupation, my father sought a better life. As a parent, he vowed to himself that through strict discipline he would instill in me a desire to learn, provide for me an education—something he never formally had—and as a result achieve success in the New World.

However, his strict ways imprinted a different mission in my young mind—like being brainwashed. Education became a top priority. Relationships with women in college were not a priority. It was as if my father was molding me in his own image to experience what he would have loved to experience in his own life—go to school, get a formal education and become a lawyer. In his crude way he guided me. And that was a powerful, driving force—following those deeply embedded principles even after his death.

Despite this, I forged my own path—achieving success and satisfaction—but still, something was missing from my life. It took a long time—and a lot of nagging feelings—before it finally became clear: a relationship with God, who had been all around me my entire life.

Beyond my father, the second person who had the greatest influence on my life was my wife, Lila Rashid Koury. Lila had been raised in a different environment than me—one of tranquility, spirituality and Christianity. It was sharply at odds with my hardscrabble upbringing of steel mills and taverns. But Lila held the key to my acceptance of God, following the way of Jesus Christ and dedicating my life to Him.

For a long time, Lila encouraged me to see the light. But I hesitated. When the Billy Graham Crusade came to Cleveland many years later, Lila urged me to attend. I finally relented. Because of this, I realized why I delayed taking such a step in my life: I was a sinner. Billy Graham convinced me that each of us is a sinner, and the only perfect person died on the Cross for our sins.

This has been my life evolution, and it says everything that needs to be said. My father was the seed—even if I didn't realize it at the time. All the things I did were because he molded and directed me. And this, unbeknownst to me, helped me navigate through life and achieve success. All the while, God was watching over me. He brought me a wonderful wife and gave me amazing children. But it was Lila who helped me realize my purpose in life: To follow in God's footsteps and help people in need. My hope is that as you read this book you begin to understand how my life was shaped, and that maybe, just maybe, as you reflect upon your own life, you will begin to realize how your life was shaped and how those around you are much more important than you often give them credit for being. At the end of each chapter I'll share a lesson I learned, sometimes unknowingly, from either my heavenly or earthly father. And maybe, just maybe, you too will learn how to go through life with a bit more humility and appreciation for the little things than you did before.

E.G. "Leo" Koury
February 2016

CHAPTER 1

Koubba, Lebanon—Life Comes Full Circle

When I was 71 years old, more than a decade after dedicating my life to Christ, and long after making peace with my father, I traveled with my wife, Lila, to my father's homeland of Lebanon. My parents, Fred and Mary Koury, never again laid eyes on Lebanon after they—along with 17 million of their countrymen—fled. Some were in search of refuge from the violence that plagued the country; others wanted to appease their gnawing hunger for a new life. The urge to visit Lebanon had nagged at me for many years, and finally, as the final year of the Biblical millennium wound its way to a conclusion, that urge became irresistible.

It was the fall of 1999, and after a lifetime of challenges I had finally gotten it right with the Lord. Despite asking for and accepting forgiveness for past sins, and carving out a new life with my family in a new city, this was the one piece of unfinished business that still needed to be addressed.

Lila and I were joined in our journey by a few relatives and our pastor. We flew to Beirut, the Paris of the Middle East. As I stood there, looking at the landscape of my ancestors for the first time in my life, I reflected on its history. After a century of strife—first foreign occupation; then later, wars—Lebanon had suffered its diaspora, a forced emigration not unlike that of the Jews who, once stateless, dispersed around the world.

For all of its sunlight, most of Lebanon is largely desolate. The sun's relentless rays stripped the land of most of its vegetation. Beyond the lush Bekaa Valley in the south there are few other places suitable for raising crops. But the Bekaa Valley was nearly a world away from the tiny village of Koubba, my family's home. With a population of only 600, the sign at the village border read "Kebba," but I always knew it as "Koubba." It didn't matter to me what the correct spelling was, as our entourage approached the village I felt immensely humbled and awed to finally have the opportunity to walk the streets where my father had walked as a child. No longer was I the son of a bootlegger within the village limits, but rather the son of Fred Koury, villager, and I had come home.

I roamed the village, eagerly soaking up stories distant relatives told about my father. He was a man of immense contradictions, and for too many years I resented him before finally overcoming the chip on my shoulder and learning to adore him. This was how it was with Fred: He was feared by those who didn't know him and revered by those who did. None of the people still living in the village had ever met my father. Rather, they had been steeped in tales from their elders about "Fred the American."

With a touch of awe, and a whole lot of gratitude, they related to our group how my father had sent money back to the village during World War II to help finance rebuilding efforts of the local church. As we listened to story after story, what struck me at my very core was how my father hadn't stepped foot in this village for more than 75 years yet many spoke of him as though he had never left and at any moment might very well walk into the room.

My father was a man with little formal education and had never held public office. Fred was a simple saloon keeper with a towering will and street shrewdness to match. Here, in his hometown, I was reminded how I was much more than the "bootlegger's son" that they considered me in Lorain from the days of my youth. It was truly amazing how after three quarters of a century he could prompt complete strangers to chase after me, compete for the right to invite me to their homes, and offer to take me to the best nightclubs and restaurants. During our visit to Koubba, it seemed as though Fred had never died, and he had never left.

It was here in this tiny, ancient village bleached by the Mediterranean sun that I found the rich heritage of which I had only been dimly aware. My grandparents spoke often of Koubba, but none of it meant much until we experienced it in person. For all of my love of family, the orbital force of family and country never felt more real to me than this moment in time. I was able to reflect upon my life as I had never been able to do before. And it was here that I realized that in my childhood and middle years, I might easily have felt rejected. I might well have worn the afflicted stamp of the shunned, dark complexion immigrant in sunny, WASPy, tow-headed America. And I might have felt the sting of social rejection and isolation. Instead, I had learned to love throughout my life simply because I was first loved as a child—by my father.

The questions washed over me: What had my whole life been about? Why did I feel driven to do everything I had done up until this moment in time?

In this country, which my famished forbearers had been forced to abandon, I had found answers.

During my life, I had done everything for my parents, especially for my dad—a man who could have been mayor, senator or even president. Fred could have been anything he wanted to be if only the cards had been dealt a little differently: If he had only received an education; if he hadn't been prematurely forced into the role of patriarch. His was a life filled with one "If only..." after another. And so, it was with immense guilt that I opened the curtains of our 11th floor balcony at the elegant Portemilio Hotel in Jounieh, near Lebanon's capital city of Beirut, and drank in the splendid view of the sea.

I was being treated as a returning prince—even though I had no right to be. The general manager, who had been tipped off by relatives of our arrival, had upgraded our room to a suite. Our traveling party was scheduled for an audience with the president of Lebanon, arranged by one of my dear friends, Ray LaHood, who served as U.S. Secretary of Transportation under President Barack Obama. Even my most distant relatives treated me as a hero—pumped full of stories about my lawyerly and political exploits over the years. Lebanese love to boast, even exaggerate a bit, about their relatives, and yet, there was guilt. My parents left their homeland by steerage passage, packed together with their countrymen like cattle and chalked like merchandise when they emerged from the ship that had carried them to their new life. I felt a sense of shame about how much better I was treated on this return trip that they never had the opportunity to make. Plus, what had I really done to deserve this level of treatment?

Later, when I shared these feelings with a kindly member of Parliament, Nabil Boustany, he looked at me with his deep eyes and smiled.

"Don't feel bad," he said. "Your father is living through you. You're living his life the way he would have wanted it to be."

This was a curious, even chilling, echo of what my father's friend had told me nearly a half-century earlier when I hovered over his casket, inconsolable: "He's really not dead; he lives on in all you do."

These days, I'm often overcome with emotion as I think about how my life has taken impossibly fortuitous turns. I'm given to wondering whether I've dreamed part of it or if everything is true. But then, before I can wrestle with my conscience, God always pulls me back, crashing down to earth and reminding me about my daily struggles with humility, salvation and the gravitational pull of my old ways. The old Leo raises his head from time to time as I treat some inconsequential slight or indignity with that old familiar growling temperament rather than the new-found spiritual patience I've learned. Gratefully, I've learned how to tamp down the old ego and pride that I'd let run wild in my younger days. The stories of my past are filled with incidents where I lacked humility and failed to be humble—lessons I'm learning from Him. The simple, unavoidable truth is that I'm in need of constant Bible study and prayer, lest I return to my sinful old ways. After all, I am my father's child—a bootlegger's son.

Leo's Lesson Learned:
If I had accepted God as part of my life when I was younger, I'd have recognized that every day is a gift and a blessing.

CHAPTER 2

Defining Moment

For years, the name Billy Graham, like the word Christianity, was familiar but not terribly important. As I struggled through an early life as the son of Lebanese immigrants in the rough-and-tumble Depression-era steel town of Lorain, Ohio, I didn't give much thought to the Christian message. I was too busy trying to stay out of harm's way while largely growing up in my father's saloon, surrounded by brawlers, drugs and prostitutes. Somehow, this boot-legger's son got an education, then made it through law school and military service before slowly building a thriving law practice and immersing myself in charity work and politics. All of this culminat-ed in my proudest achievement—helping Jimmy Carter get elected to the White House.

But there had been little time in all that flurry of activity to reflect on the Lord's Divine whisper—even if it had been there all along, quietly speaking to me. It wouldn't have mattered anyway back then. My pride would have gotten in the way. Because of my tough upbringing, I had developed not so much a chip on my shoulder, but a full-fledged log. That's not to say that there weren't constant reminders of the Lord's call, just that I paid them no heed. And that kept me from seeing the world in the proper context—especially the world of my father.

The signs were always there. People were all around me for a rea-son—but I never opened my eyes and saw what was right in front of me. Almost everyone in my grandparents' generation, from my grandfather Isaac on down, had a name from the Old Testament. While I go by Leo, my real first name is Elias, a version of the Bib-lical prophet Elijah. I can still see my maternal grandmother, with a cigarette dangling from her mouth and an infant clinging to her apron, reading her Bible. Somehow, through a thousand life trials and numerous close brushes with death, I always emerged intact. And yet, like a blind man who declines an opportunity to regain his vision, I never really saw God's hand at work in my uncanny good fortune. That's because I lacked humility and had not yet learned the importance of being humble.

Then there was the biggest influence of all, my wife Lila, a fervent believer who gently prodded me toward Christ for years. She never gave up hope that I might change my ways. For most of my life, however, those influences lay dormant as I chased worldly success in politics, business and the law. And then, suddenly, and certainly inexplicably, at the age of 65 I was somehow compelled to attend the Billy Graham Crusade. And the world as I knew it changed. Everything I had known before suddenly became clear—bathed in a different light.

It was 1994, and the famous preacher's visit to Cleveland was the result of a crusade waged by a retired Cleveland banker and devout Christian named Gordon Heffern.

Gordon had set his mind on convincing the Billy Graham Evangelistic Association to schedule a crusade in Cleveland. For a long time, people ridiculed Gordon's ambition, but he remained undaunted. Eventually, after almost a decade of working behind the scenes, Gordon's efforts bore fruit: The Rev. Graham was scheduled to arrive for a five-night crusade in June 1994 at Cleveland Municipal Stadium, the former cavernous sports stadium on the shores of Lake Erie.

To this day, I'm not sure what made me attend. The best way to explain it is that I simply felt led to hear his message. And, as my wife and I entered the stadium that first evening, I had the urge to get as close as possible to the action.

At my prompting, we worked our way down near the front, ignoring a guard who tried to direct us elsewhere.

"This area is reserved," he said.

"Yeah, for me," I shot back before pushing ahead with my wife.

As the Rev. Graham spoke that evening in his familiar lilting baritone, the message of Christian redemption began to make sense for the first time in my life. What had always felt like a thinly veiled accusation, like a personal condemnation of my sinfulness, instead now felt like a loving invitation to change my life for the better. Here was Billy Graham—a name synonymous with Christian preaching, a world-famous adviser to nearly a dozen presidents and a man who's been called the American pope—distilling his message into simple direct language that touched my heart.

Repenting doesn't mean you're bad, he explained. It simply means you want to change your life.

Those words shook me to the core.

Suddenly, the familiar passage in the Book of John about being born again came alive as never before: It's impossible to enter the kingdom of God except by the Holy Spirit, by being born again. I felt as though the Rev. Graham was personally tapping me on the shoulder, gently prodding my understanding with a few simple, kind words.

"Son, here's the clarity," he seemed to be telling me. And, for the first time in my long life, this message of Christ's redemption seemed so very clear. Graham was breaking down my stubbornness and softening my ego by explaining how to embrace the Lord's message rather than simply lecturing on why we should do it. In his own way, he was melting down my lifelong ignorance of God's grace and opening my eyes. And so, my heart was ready when Graham invited those who wanted to accept Christ as their Savior to come forward and bear personal witness.

"I'm going to ask you to get up out of your seat and come stand in front of the platform here," he intoned to the crowd.

Without really thinking about it, I began to get up. My wife, evidently shocked, asked me, "Where are you going?"

"I want to hear more," was all I could think to tell her.

Moments later, I found myself on my knees before 65,000 people in an ancient, windblown horseshoe stadium accepting Christ into my life as my personal Savior. It was a defining moment in my life.

As I made my way back to my chair, I was accosted by a local television reporter, Lorrie Taylor. She wanted my reaction to what I had just done.

At first, I declined. After all, I was trying desperately to make sense of what had just happened myself. I hardly felt in a position to describe it for strangers.

"It's personal," I said. "I'm not trying to impress anyone. I can't even explain it."

"Why not?" she goaded. "Are you ashamed? You just witnessed before 65,000 people."

She had a point, and so I talked a little into her microphone, trying somehow to explain what had just happened.

"I definitely feel the spirit in my heart," I said, the camera rolling. "But it wasn't just the people here. I felt I was alone; alone in my communication with God, opening my heart and my eyes to my obligations, and I hope that I could be a better person."

"Did you leave here a different man?" she asked.

"Yes," I replied. "No doubt about it. Humbled for the first time. That's hard to say for a lawyer."

I told her that when I heard about everybody being a sinner, and that I was one of them, it connected with me. If I confessed my sin, I'd be forgiven.

"Everybody's a sinner," I said. "The only perfect person is Jesus Christ."

As I finished talking, the camera light went off. I noticed Lorrie was nearly crying.

"What's the matter?" I asked her. "Did I offend you?"

"No. Something happened to you, and I don't know what it is, but it's affecting me, too."

As if the day's events weren't indicative enough of God's powerful presence in the stadium that day, I would soon learn an additional detail that would leave me in a humble state of spiritual awe. Though I didn't know it at the time, both my son and my daughter were also in the stadium, accepting the Lord into their respective lives. Two of my four children had somehow independently heard the same divine whisper that I did and arrived at the same place that day to hear the same message of spiritual rebirth in the Lord.

About five days later, I was in my office when my secretary alerted me that a TV camera crew was waiting outside and wanted to speak with me. I walked out and there was Lorrie Taylor with her cameraman.

"What are you doing here?" I asked.

"I wanted to see if you changed."

"No, I didn't."

Lorrie invited me to lunch. She said she wanted to talk about how my Billy Graham experience affected me. I accepted her offer.

Over lunch that day, I told her I was a sinner.

"Billy Graham gave the right message," I explained. "We're all sinners. Everybody feels guilty but nobody wants to be judged. Yet, Christ never judges anyone."

I never saw Lorrie again in person after that lunch. But it didn't matter. After many years of living one kind of life, I was heading—being pulled, actually—down a long corridor toward another life. Because of my new relationship with God, nothing in my life would ever be the same again—including how I saw the legacy of my father and what he truly meant to me.

Leo's Lesson Learned:

When you open your heart and eyes, you will discover the endless possibilities that appear before you.

CHAPTER 3

Countries

To understand me and who I am, you need to understand my father and who he was. Born in 1903 in Koubba, Lebanon, Fred Isaac Koury had the bad luck to come of age when the Ottoman Empire was occupying his small country with brutal force. There was little opportunity to find work, and children quit school early to help earn money for their families. It was a miserable time.

While Lebanon is known for its sunny, moderate climate along the scenic Mediterranean coast, this has become something of a curse for its people. The sun shines all but about 50 to 60 days each year, which has created a country of extremes—luscious fruit in some regions; barren land in others. Wrestling a living from this living dichotomy has been difficult for centuries, which perhaps accounts for the fact that the Lebanese and their forebears, the Phoenicians, made a name for themselves as world-renowned traders and merchants instead of traditional farmers.

For centuries, this country—the size of Rhode Island—has been at the crossroads of the Middle East, a land teeming with as many as a dozen, often warring, religious groups. Among Christian denominations, there are Roman Catholics, Maronites and Eastern Orthodox. There are also Muslims, Druze, Shiites and Sunnis. The close proximity of so many disparate peoples has proven to be a recipe for volatility and ceaseless strife for centuries.

To further complicate the Lebanese plight, the country often was overrun by stronger invaders. Following Turkish rule in the 20th century through World War I, there was a French mandate for Lebanon and Syria. More recently still, the neighboring Israelis sought to dominate the country so as to ensure that Lebanon would serve as a security buffer between itself and its bitter Muslim enemies.

My grandfather, Isaac Koury, grew up in this environment and set out to make a better life for his family. He emigrated from Lebanon to the United States around 1896 and became a peddler of dry goods.

In the years that followed, he made numerous trips back and forth across the Atlantic Ocean between the U.S. and Lebanon, trying to engineer the process of moving his family to America. But it took years to save enough money to make a difference. In his absence, my father assumed the role of family backbone—even though he had an older brother, Alex, who was more of an adventurer than provider.

Despite this burden, no obstacle prevented my father from providing for his family. At age 11 he stole boots from Turkish soldiers and sold them on the black market to buy flour so his mother could bake bread. In doing that, he braved a severe penalty: It was well known that Turkish soldiers would either emasculate or cut off the hands of any boy who was caught stealing. My father knew it was wrong to steal, but at the time believed that sometimes in the most desperate moments of the most desperate situations you do what you have to do in order to survive. As Fred got older and began to build a life in America he gained a new understanding of the world: You should not break the law no matter what. There is a clear difference between doing what's right and what's wrong.

This early responsibility came with a high cost: My father didn't get to know what it was like to graduate from school. Instead, he became a master of the school of hard knocks. Adapting to survive does that to you. It hardens you while instilling a sense of responsibility and eventually eliminating moral ambiguity. It's not easy to get your moral compass back on track—but my father did. As he got older, it crystallized, led by honesty and integrity—two traits he passed down and instilled in me. He did not, however, know how to say "I love you," which gnawed at me for years. And it became my quest to discover whether any feelings of love for me existed under his crusty exterior. After I came to Christ, I realized God was always there for me, and even in the form of my father, he was always looking out for me and guiding my life. I also came to recognize that my father's inability to utter those three words came from no one ever saying them to him. But that never detracted from the good man he was at his core.

With this base character firmly in place, with the Turks firmly and brutally in control of Lebanon, and Fred's family nearly destitute, my

father left his homeland in the early 1920s to seek o'
everyone. After a few stumbles, he eventually landeᵤ
steel town of Lorain, Ohio, where his grandfather's cousᵢ
ventured years earlier, and where my grandfather, Isaac, was ᵥ
out a living.

Fred was 18 or 19 years old when he arrived in the U.S. He couldn't
speak English and had only an elementary school education. At first,
he was turned away, and ended up in Mexico. Back then, if you had
eye disease or a communicable disease, immigration officials rejected you. The actual cause of my father's rejection isn't known, but it's
a story that has been handed down in our family—how my father
entered the U.S. through Mexico. In the 1920s, Mexico and the U.S.
shared an open border—travel between the two countries was much
easier than it is today, and with a lot less drama. The details of my
father's adventure are a bit sketchy but I think that he went to Mexico, then crossed the border and made his way to Lorain, where other
members of his family were living. He subsequently went to live with
his father.

Years later, I asked my father why he decided to leave the country
of his birth.

A man of few words, he replied, "Because I was hungry."

My mother, Mary Hanna Koury, arrived in the U.S. in September
1913. She had a far different experience than my father. She once told
me a story about how, upon her arrival at Ellis Island, she and other
Lebanese children were separated for hours from the adults in their
party. They were left to fend for themselves in alien surroundings,
none of them knowing a word of English. It was a harrowing experience that left an indelible impression.

Mary's uncle, Elias Hanna, escorted her to the U.S. They arrived
with several other family members, including children. Mary was
about 10 years old. She had a self-reliant nature, and it wasn't long before she became a surrogate mother for her younger siblings—Henry
and William, her brothers; and Henrietta and Wilma, her sisters.

There is little doubt that Mary had a rough early life—not only did
she have to mother her siblings, but she also had to work in order
to help the family make ends meet. She worked at the Yellow Cab

xi service with her cousin Rose. She shined shoes. Sometimes, she even worked as a cashier. Mary did everything she could to pitch in. As a result, Mary's mother, Louise Hanna, treated her like a partner because she worked in the family business. An unfortunate consequence was that she wasn't raised—or loved—like a daughter.

Despite this, Mary became a wonderful mother. She was very loving and nurturing—but she didn't spoil us. She left the spoiling to my grandfather, Isaac. My mother used to tell me that I was stubborn, which I was convinced I learned from her. One time, she tried to teach me how to bake Syrian bread.

I said, "I can't. I'm a boy. I don't have to do this."

My mother didn't let me off the hook so easily.

"Yes, you'll do it," she said. "You'll learn."

She was a hard woman to oppose. So I learned how to put the bread in the oven and then, when it was done, take it out.

Looking back, my mother was raised much like my father was. Nobody ever told either of them that they loved them. They were given responsibility and let loose upon the world. In Mary's case, that meant going to school through the eighth grade and then going to work full time. She became a grown-up long before she should have been one. But she adapted—that's what you did back then.

As for my father, in Lorain Fred was placed in school at a fourth or fifth grade level—even though he was nearly an adult. In those days, they didn't have remedial courses such as English as a Second Language. This humiliated Fred so much that he didn't want to attend. He quit school and entered the workforce, taking an assortment of jobs to make ends meet.

This, however, wasn't the end of my father's education. He was driven to succeed, and my mother remembered him attending night school after they were married. She also told me he used to read everything he could get his hands on. He was interested in world events, and one of his favorite magazines was *U.S. News & World Report*. Beyond being interesting, the magazine also allowed my father to continue to practice his English. Over the course of his life, he continued to read a lot of different materials, which probably is the source of my love of reading. He even used books to teach himself how to be a better businessman. For years he kept a dog-eared copy of Dale Carnegie's "How to Win Friends and Influence People" on the nightstand next to his bed.

All of this was a gradual process. So while he had arrived in America, things weren't all that much easier for him. But he took solace in knowing there was freedom from the Turks and a better opportunity to make something of himself. At first, he sold dry goods and clothing door-to-door, picking up the same occupation as his father. He would go on to own taverns.

Although my father was a hard worker, he was no saint. While he tried to demonstrate honesty and integrity through his actions, it wasn't always easy. Often, the challenges he faced in his life bubbled to the surface to create a constant struggle between doing what he knew was right and what his emotions urged him to do. He was a man of tremendous emotional volatility and pent-up anger. When he came home each evening, the kids scattered. You could feel the tension in the house rise in anticipation of his short fuse. Today, I can see that he was frustrated over never having had a childhood and being forced into the role of primary family breadwinner at too early an age. In middle age, he was still the patriarch of a now very extended family. This wore on him and made him resentful.

My father was a prideful man, and had a way about him. It was something he was born with. As an adult, he stood only 5 feet 9 inches. He was overweight, close to 220 pounds. And he wasn't physically imposing. He had soft hands, which indicated a lack of strength. But he would look at you with his eyes—eyes of integrity—and nothing else would matter. Even in the most volatile moments, his true self shone through his eyes. But giants were afraid of him.

Fred's titanic energy and uncommon generosity for those in need served him well. He combined those two traits to create unique opportunities in the working-class, immigrant-choked town of Lorain during the first half of the century. When the legendary World War II OSS head "Wild Bill" Donovan came to Lorain to try to organize the U.S. Steel plant for the steelworkers' union after the war, my dad supplied a meeting place, just as he would offer new arrivals to the plant a room and meals while they got settled into their new job. Years of such favors would later translate into real political power.

Much of this activity floated on rivers of whiskey that my father supplied in his three saloons, all located near the giant U.S. Steel plant on East 28th Street. When the workers received their pay every two weeks, the good times rolled. It went on like that even as Prohibition ruled the country in the 1920s. The only change was that higher quality, but still illicit whiskey from Canada increasingly replaced the rotgut liquor made in thousands of illegal basement stills. The good stuff was shipped across Lake Erie by rumrunners who often evaded the U.S. Coast Guard. Thirsty lakefront towns, such as Lorain, received more than their share of the bounty. While my father didn't own a tavern until the late 1930s, his experience selling bootleg whiskey was seasoned by then.

In time, all of this caught up to my dad. In 1935, he was convicted of tax violations connected with selling bootleg alcohol during Prohibition, and he was shipped off to federal prison in Lewisburg, Pennsylvania.

After he had served his time and was preparing to return home, he told my mother that when he came back he was going to treat her the best he could because she had stood by him—with no hesitation. Some of my father's cohorts, who were in prison with him, had changed their colors and started giving up names. My father was irate with them, especially since he had given them work during Prohibition. He kept his mouth shut and refused to implicate anyone else. He told my mother to pick him up at an earlier train station stop so he could get off and avoid the cohorts who were released at the same time he was. Our entire family showed up at that earlier train stop. And when my father got off the train, he scooped up my sister and off we went—away from the people whom my father had served his jail time with. He really did not want them to follow us.

Because he had mutely taken his punishment, my father returned from his brief prison stay as a community hero. His time behind bars served him well and taught him a great many things. Among them, he told me not to fear being approached by crime figures who wanted to form alliances.

"Son, don't be afraid," he said. "I learned in federal prison, if you refuse them honorably, they won't bother you. But if you take anything from them, they'll kill you if you don't produce."

During his entire life, my father never took anything from them—and he always remained his own man.

Some people even started calling my father the unofficial mayor of South Lorain or the "Mayor of Pearl Avenue." Despite his lack of ever holding political office, in time my father's reputation—as well as all the favors he had done—helped him and a friend, an iron-fisted Hungarian lawyer named Joe Ujhelyi, build a powerful Democratic political machine in Lorain County. Ujhelyi would go on to serve as county party chairman for more than 40 years, the longest in Ohio's history.

Of course, the incumbent local political and business establishment didn't cede power and influence gracefully. They attacked my father every way they could, though to little avail. The more they savaged him, the more highly regarded he became among South Lorain's working-class immigrants. Fred Koury had become something of a folk hero.

When my father died years later at the age of 47, I was crushed. I never really understood back then what was going on around me—especially with my father. I knew he was important. I knew he was tough. And I knew he had a hard time showing any love for me. But that did little to soften the blow. I had just completed my first year of law school, and now I wanted to quit. It was my father, after all, who had calmly talked me through my initial law school jitters after I called him a few weeks in, convinced that I couldn't hold up to the punishing competition for grades.

Still, I refused to cry over my father's death. Instead, I mutely stood like a stone before his coffin for three days, mostly ignoring the kind words offered by well-wishers and not realizing that God was all around me. Instead, I was lost and empty.

Finally, a friend of my dad, a man whom the family had known for years, offered some of the wisest counsel I've ever received.

"He's not really dead," he said. "He lives on in you and all you do. Just uphold his name."

And from that day on, that's precisely what I tried to do. Long before I came to form a relationship with God, He was already all around me, speaking to me through all the wonderful people who provided support in my life. As a result, living up to my father's name became the central organizing principle for nearly everything I did over the next 40 years. My life would become a love story dedicated to him—even if I didn't truly understand the ramifications of it at the time—and it would lay the foundation for my eventual recognition of my relationship with God.

Leo's Lesson Learned:
Do what you must to survive and uphold your father's name.

CHAPTER 4
Friends

It is a little ironic that the name "Koury" in Arabic means "family of priests." My grandfather, Isaac, had brothers named Abraham and Jacob, which were all Biblical names, and all priests. But you'd think because of that, my father wouldn't have turned a rather deaf ear to absorbing any religious training. In some ways, I think he just took to the streets like a lost boy. Maybe that was a way to avoid my grandfather, who was very strict. The two got into frequent loud arguments, but afterward, they were the best of friends.

The city my father would eventually call home was similar in many respects to his native country. Lorain was home to people from as many as 55 nationality groups, most of whom settled there for work in the booming steel plant. Back then it was called National Tube and was a division of Andrew Carnegie's giant U.S. Steel, the world's first billion-dollar corporation. With company recruiters crisscrossing Europe to recruit mill hands, thousands of immigrants from the continent were eventually persuaded to uproot themselves for a new life in America and a job in the sprawling plant situated on 1,400 acres along Lorain's Black River.

For decades, these new arrivals and their offspring converted millions of tons of salmon-colored Minnesota iron ore into stainless steel rails and later steel tubing for pipelines. The giant blast furnaces in Lorain were fired up around the clock, producing as much as one-seventh of U.S. Steel's mammoth output at one point. So hungry for steel was America in the first half of the 20th century that even the Great Depression caused only a minor slowdown in production.

Poles comprised Lorain's largest ethnic group, but there were also so many Hungarians that the neighborhood around the mill was quickly dubbed "Little Budapest." There were also lots of Italians, Czechs, Romanians, Greeks and Germans who had moved to Lorain. By the 1920s, African-Americans were migrating from the South, and Mexican immigrants had begun the move north from

Texas. Later still, desperately poor "hillbillies" arrived from rural Appalachia. And soon after World War II, as many as 18,000 Puerto Ricans were added to the mix. Lorain was truly a melting pot.

All these people needed dry goods—clothes, needles and thread, blankets, tablecloths—anything that might be needed for the home. And the Lebanese, one of the smallest ethnic communities in Lorain, were eager to provide them.

Isaac was a peddler. He would take his horse and buggy to Cleveland's Bolivar Road neighborhood, where a wealthy Lebanese merchant named Joseph Hanna would sell these goods to people like my grandfather, who then sold them door-to-door, sometimes in places as far away as Sandusky. It proved profitable enough because somehow my grandfather found the means to donate to the building fund at St. George Antiochian Orthodox Church in the 1930s—the church in Cleveland to which I still belong today.

In 1920, as Prohibition took root in the country with the introduction of the Volstead Act, these Lebanese peddlers began to add a new item to their array of offerings: pint bottles of bootleg whiskey. Even my saintly grandmother Anna took part in the family trade.

Anna loved to smoke cigarettes; that was her pleasure. I can still recall her reading her Arabic Bible, a cigarette dangling from her lips—and sometimes a grandchild perched in her arms—pausing to take care of thirsty customers. When a man would come to the door, she'd climb up a ladder to the attic, bring down a pint or two in her apron, and make a sale to the stranger. At the time, no one could have imagined how much pain and dislocation engaging in this illicit trade would later bring to my family.

By the age of 19, my father, always a decisive sort, declared that he needed a wife. In the tightly knit Lebanese community, that was quickly arranged. His grandmother and my mother's grandmother went to work in typical matchmaking fashion of their time.

My mother was living in Louisville, Kentucky, at that time, but her grandmother in Lorain interceded. A trip to Kentucky for my dad to meet my mother, the former Mary Hanna, was arranged. She was a year older than him. He decided he liked what he saw, and they went to get a marriage license.

That could have been the end of the story, but it wasn't. Things get a bit more complicated. My father, as it turned out, was on some kind of mission to claim his bride right away. While telling Mary that they were only applying for a license, my dad and his mother-in-law-to-be ensured they were actually married by a justice of the peace at the same time.

My father was smart about this. He knew Mary's relatives would make trouble and other people would stick their noses into the matter. He anticipated they would ask, "What are you marrying him for? He's a greenhorn, he just came over…you're educated." This is because my mother had more years of schooling than my dad.

Word got out about the secret marriage, and Mary's relatives started to meddle. They asked questions and got everyone worked up. As a result, my mother said she wasn't going to marry my father. She was so upset that she had been legally married without her knowledge that she tore up the marriage license. She wanted a real wedding—done right.

At the time, there was a standing religious rule that during Lent no marriages could be held. Today, some Catholic churches continue to forbid it. So my father and mother waited until after Lent was over. They moved to Lorain to live with my grandparents, and my mother was able to have a traditional church wedding. Everyone ended up happy.

In 1925, Mary gave birth to their first child, my brother Michael. Three years later, I was born. And three years after that came my little sister Joan.

As with all family members, my dad was pretty tough with my mother. If she wanted to do something, she didn't listen to his orders not to at first, but she learned. She was stubborn, but eventually became less obstinate.

The funny part of all of this was that despite the strictness, despite the toughness, I never had the urge to run away from home. I was an ornery cuss because my grandfather spoiled me so much, and I was a benevolent brat. Remember, I hadn't even come close to learning how to be humble.

One time, when I was 14 years old, I wasn't particularly happy with my father and decided to stand up for my mother against him. You see, women liked my dad; he was good-looking. Sometimes my mother would accuse him of indiscretions and he would reply, "You're crazy." And then she'd say something else, and he would try to intimidate her.

On this occasion I grabbed a knife and stood in front of my mother. "Don't touch her," I said.

My father looked at me, and then just started laughing. He didn't get mad. He just laughed. Deep inside, he was proud of me that I stood up for my mother—even if he thought she was wrong. Everyone else in the family backed off, but not me. I was my father's son; a reincarnation of him.

Another thing my father was not used to was having his own father around. He was bullheaded and did whatever he wanted. This created a lot of strife between the two, and they would argue constantly and even hit each other at times. But, after they stopped fighting, they became like sugar and honey. That's how people fought in the old country tradition—you got used to it. My mother would say, "Oh, leave them alone. They'll be alright." And they were.

My sister Joan remembers being very afraid of my father when she was young. Joan and I became very close because I was like a father to her.

"My mother would scare us by saying I'm going to tell your father," she recalls. "Everybody would faint when she would say that. And he never hit us because he didn't have to; we were so afraid."

That's because when my father came into the house all he had to do was look at us. He had that look about him that said he meant business. He never touched us. But he also never said, "I love you"—to any of us in the family. It must have been part of that male bravado he carried with him—the attitude and look. Interestingly enough, everybody said I had that very same look every time I walked in the courtroom. Little did I realize at the time that it was because my father had shaped me in his own image.

Our family lived in South Lorain for the first few years of my life. South Lorain was a gritty, working-class neighborhood. It grew up in the shadow of the steel mill's main gate at Pearl Avenue and East 28th Street, almost from the day the mill began operating in 1895. By conventional middle-class standards, it was no nirvana. The neighborhood was full of rough characters, and all the crime and vice one might care to see. Still, I thought it was a splendid place to grow up because you tended to cluster around your own ethnic group, while also mixing with the other nationality groups that were so close in proximity to each other. As the Nobel Prize-winning author Toni Morrison would later write about her hometown:

> There were lots and lots of immigrants. In Lorain at that time, there were Mexicans for the steel, southern people from the hills, destitute—mind you, I'm born in 1928, and that means Depression. And then, of course, there were middle-class people… We had poor neighborhoods, but I never lived in the house that wasn't next to a white family. Of course, we never thought of them as white, we thought of them in their nationalities: Greeks, Italians, Irish, Jews…what bound us was class. We lived in an income strata, not a racial ghetto.

But by the simple nature of its physical layout, Lorain had a problem with its residents—however well they got along—that it could never quite overcome. The city is shaped like a long tunnel rather than an area that comes together in a central core. Its very geography worked against building a natural sense of community, you might say. And it was in this long tunnel of the town that at age 5 I had the first of what would be several near-brushes with death. All of these incidents would later help me to realize that the hand of God was upon me my entire life, though I scarcely knew it at the time.

The first one happened like this: A bunch of us kids were playing in a neighbor's yard when one girl challenged us to light a fire. Someone did, and the group began to dance around it. I foolishly jumped over the small blaze, catching my pants on fire. I began screaming, and 16-year-old Vic King, a neighbor playing nearby, came running. He quickly put out the fire, but not before I'd been badly burned. Like all adults of that era, my mother, who had come running when she heard my screams, applied butter to the burns. But she never imagined that wouldn't help and instead made matters worse.

For almost a year after that incident I was in and out of the hospital, shuttled from one doctor to another. At first, the prognosis was catastrophic—that I would lose both legs. Then, the doctors thought I would merely be a cripple for the rest of my life. In the end, though, a miracle came to pass: I regained the full use of both legs.

After one particular nasty argument concerning how my father was treating his injured son, my grandfather took me to live with him and my grandmother. I spent nearly a year with them. They felt so sorry for my condition that they spoiled me rotten. I was practically given full adult status. All the old Lebanese would sit around a bench outside our old two-story building and talk about the old country and different things, and I was the only kid there. It was an interesting period in my life.

One time, my grandfather's sister, who was matriarchal and smart, said to my grandfather in Arabic, "You're spoiling that boy. What's he doing here with us?"

Grandpa Isaac said, "Shut up. This boy's going to be somebody."

That's what he would tell his sister. Nobody held me accountable. Instead, they continued to spoil me, deflecting attention from my behavior. Unfortunately, nobody taught me the importance of humility.

My grandfather didn't speak much English, couldn't make a living, wasn't very bright and argued with his son all the time. But he was good to me and would take me along while he sold dry goods door to door. He'd say, "Missus, buy something from me." That's all he could say, but he could count money. When lunchtime came, he'd take me to a delicatessen and buy me a salami sandwich and a bottle of pop. And, he even put me under a tree.

I fondly recall—and I've even relived this in my dreams—the little boy I once was with the burn on my legs, sitting propped under that tree, gazing up lovingly at my dear indulging Grandpa Isaac, who had just offered me a hunk of bread and a loving pat on the head.

"Koul ya eineh," he said.

"What's that mean, Grandpa?"

"Eat, my darling," he explained.

There's nothing in life but love.

Life, however, didn't smile as brightly on the boy whose quick response saved my life. Just six months after my accident and his brush with heroism, Vic King was driving his Ford convertible when it rolled over, immediately killing him. For a long time afterward, I struggled with his death and the guilt it engendered within me. Why did I live and he die? He was older and stronger than I was. In the end, I could arrive at only one conclusion—the Lord was looking out for me.

By 1935, things were otherwise looking up for our family. My father's hard work was paying off. We had recently moved to a larger house in central Lorain with more middle-class neighbors. It felt like a real step up from South Lorain, which was just a few blocks away. But fate can be cruel. Prohibition had ended in 1933, but the government was still pursuing bootleggers for tax evasion charges. My father, other family members, and probably all the Lebanese merchants sold bootleg whiskey to make ends meet during the Depression. This included the Lebanese from Lorain, Cleveland, Canton, Youngstown and other surrounding areas. All of them had gone to the Lebanese enclave on Bolivar Road in Cleveland to get their wholesale groceries and dry goods. The whiskey they bought for resale came from Canada. And my dad and grandfather had first sold the liquor in the Hungarian community, which is how we were acquainted with the Hungarians and became close associates and friends. As the bootleg business grew, my father expanded his reach, selling whiskey to many different people around Lorain. And that created a wide net for the government to pursue.

So when law enforcement cracked down, everyone got caught: my grandfather, my grandmother, my uncle and my dad. My grandfather, however, was let off the hook when my Uncle George took the fall for him. And they were all convicted and sentenced to the federal prison in Lewisburg, Pennsylvania.

I was about 7 years old at the time, and I remember when they were taking my father away to prison. We went to see him at the U.S. Marshal's office before he was to leave. There was a glass partition, but I could hear what was said. I'll never forget it.

The officer said, "Koury,"—not mister, not Fred—"all you have to do is sing like a bird," meaning turn over the names of those officials and others who were being bribed to allow bootlegging.

But that's what hit me: "Sing like a bird and you won't go anywhere."

My father spit in the officer's face, and the marshal backhanded him right in the face. That's when I started screaming. My mother later told me I was inconsolable because I completely lost it when the officer hit my dad. I went berserk because I couldn't get to him.

Dad received a sentence of nine months to a year. But the stigma of having a father labeled as a bootlegger stayed with me long after he was released.

When I was in sixth grade, a school bully named Tiger taunted me as a "little son of a bootlegger." I was so enraged I let him have it with everything I had. He ended up beating me up. But I wasn't done. I returned, thinking I would catch him off-guard, but I still lost the fight. I was left to nurse both my bruised body and ego. That wouldn't be the first time my ego would get the best of me.

The task of taking care of our family while my father was in prison fell to my Uncle Alex, the adventurer. Alex had a little cigar store and had made a rough time of his life. He had a penchant for drinking and women, which often got him into trouble. In fact, it was because he shot a man in the leg while he was drunk that the family had to quickly get him out of Lebanon before anything worse happened. He went to Mexico, which was a destination for numerous Arabic immigrants, and spent time there before my grandfather urged my father to bring him to Ohio so he could be with the rest of the family.

My father was hesitant to act, but my grandfather overruled him and brought Alex to Ohio. It was unfortunate that Alex's vices kept getting him into trouble and unable to achieve his full potential. He had a good heart. But after my father went to jail he finally had his chance to make good on things by taking care of all of us—which he did for a while.

Years later, my father eventually re-assumed the role of the family patriarch from Alex, which among other matters, included marrying off my aunts Julia and Sally, and later my Uncle George. My father took care of all of them—my grandparents and everyone else. Five families. It was a great responsibility. And watching it taught me the importance of family. It was a lesson I would never forget.

Leo's Lesson Learned:

Family takes care of family—no matter what happens.

CHAPTER 5

People

It was called, appropriately enough, Mill Tavern. From the front door, you could toss a stone and hit the main gate of the huge steel mill that had built South Lorain's economy. When quitting time arrived for thousands of thirsty mill hands, they didn't have to walk far to quench their thirst—just down Pearl Avenue, between East 28th and East 29th streets. And for much of my formative years Mill Tavern would serve as a focal point of activity.

From the first day the steel mill furnaces were lit late in the 19th century, the workers shuffled out at day's end and made a beeline for the nearest spot to tip back a few bottles. My dad had the prime spot for the saloon, and over the next several years he would add two more locations. In the early 1930s, after Prohibition ended, Mill Tavern was licensed as just a beer and wine joint. In the late 1930s, after my dad returned from the penitentiary, it received a full liquor license.

Mill Tavern was registered in my mother's name. My dad's prison record rendered him ineligible to hold a liquor license. As a matter of fact, most everything was in my mother's name. And she became very protective of this arrangement. One time, years later when my father wanted to buy a car, he decided to put it in his name. My mother thought that was a terrible idea and threw a fit.

"What are you going to do? Start putting things in your name now? No!" she said. My father was tough, but my mother was tough, too, and she wouldn't let him get away with ideas like that, which she knew could have negative consequences.

Contrasting Mill Tavern's grungy feel—with an equally working-class clientele—was my father's impeccable appearance. While at work, he would wear a Stetson hat, Stetson shoes and a Hart Schaffner Marx suit. It was a look you couldn't miss when you were in the tavern because he stood out. He had such beautiful wavy, black hair, but even when it was hot he always wore the hat.

Above Mill Tavern my dad had several rooms that he rented to Hispanics and other immigrant workers from the steel plant. This served as an additional way to generate money beyond the tavern.

Next door was my Uncle George's cigar store and pool hall. Uncle George was a stoutly built, former middleweight boxing champion who once was nicknamed "Dynamite Dunn." Uncle George's Golden Gloves championship was stripped after it was discovered he had accepted $7 for winning an amateur fight. That didn't diminish Uncle George's stature. With him around, there was no need for bouncers. If anyone got out of line, Uncle George would take care of the troublemaker.

Mill Tavern was our family's cash cow. Every other Friday, which was pay day at the mill, my dad would get up early to open shop. Sometimes, he even slept in his car or on the pool table because the tavern stayed open until 2 a.m. and he thought it was easier than coming home and resetting for the next day. When he did come home, my father would put his old-fashioned alarm clock in the bathroom and set it to ring at 4 or 4:30 a.m. He would get up, get dressed, and then lug a big bankroll of cash to the tavern so he could cash the workers' checks. Mill hands seemingly always lived paycheck to paycheck, so my father recognized if he could cash those checks on payday at the tavern, they'd spend more of their money with him.

On Sunday, my father would sell liquor, which was a technically illegal practice, but he knew the liquor agents and as long as he was around to supervise, they left him alone.

Looking back, I never really appreciated the hard work and dedication my father put into his businesses to put food on our table. But luckily, he instilled his work ethic in my brother Mike and me—even if I didn't notice it at the time. Because of this, Mill Tavern became our prep school. It was our first real taste of the world of work, adults and politics. It's where I learned how to talk to people and get along with them—skills that would serve me well later in life, including as an attorney. My father was my teacher. He loved greetings and talked the language of the customer. Never was this on greater display then when someone sauntered up to the bar.

For example, when a Hungarian would come in, he'd say, "Hogy vagy?" When a Polish man came in, he'd welcome them with, "Jak się masz?"

I started copying my dad, learning just enough of nearly a dozen languages so that I could banter with the customers and make them feel like personal guests. It was classic Dale Carnegie tactics, meeting people on their own terms and making them comfortable.

It worked. The clientele was loyal, and it grew.

My tenure at Mill Tavern did not start so happily. It was the mid-1940s, and I was in high school. Unbeknownst to my father, I was becoming a pretty fair athlete, despite my serious leg burns from years before. My dad learned about my sports career secondhand, when he happened upon an account of my achievements one day in the local newspaper.

"What's this?" he demanded, confronting me with the article.

"Sports," I replied.

"Sports are for Americans," he said. "You get your a-- on a bus and come down here after school and work."

I couldn't believe my ears. He was ordering me to quit playing sports, my greatest joy. I cried bitterly, but of course obeyed. I resented him for years afterward.

My first job consisted of racking balls in the pool room, restocking the Coke machine and mopping up the floor. Gradually, as my dad became comfortable with my work and level of responsibility, he let me run the place for entire days while he was away.

Though I didn't understand it at the time, and I certainly didn't appreciate it, my father was teaching me through his actions what a good work ethic really was. I was just an angry kid who was mad at his father. It wouldn't be until years later that I would recognize how un-Christian my behavior was—and it was pretty bad at times.

Once, when he told me to get on down to the tavern to work, I looked at him with a tear in my eye and said, "You S.O.B. I'm going to be tougher than you."

Back then, I hated him for making me forgo everything else I cared about in my life to work at his tavern. I was clearly becoming my father's son, and I was going to challenge him all the time. While all the others were afraid of him, I was not. I hadn't learned the Lord's teachings on forgiveness yet. Instead, getting even was more my style. Accordingly, I wasn't afraid to fire one of my dad's favorite waitresses just to stir things up.

It happened one day when I was about 18 years old. My father wasn't at the tavern that day and had left me in charge. He was a fanatic for cleanliness. The waitress spilled some beer on the floor and didn't clean it up. She even walked right over it, not giving it a second glance.

I caught her attention and said, "Hey, Rose, would you please clean that up?"

Then I went back to my work and didn't think about it until 10 minutes later, when I noticed that not only had Rose not cleaned up the mess but was walking right over it again—ignoring it as though it weren't there.

"Rose," I said, "I thought I told you to clean this up?"

And that's when she gave me some lip.

"I don't have to listen to you, you little s---," she said. "You're not my boss."

That was it. She was history.

"Oh, I'm not?" I said. "You're fired."

And then Rose grabbed her coat, which was on a hanger, and took a swing at my face.

I dodged it, then escorted her out of the building. As I said, I wasn't very Christian-like back then.

"I'm going to the prosecutor!" she screamed. "You're not even supposed to be in here. You're illegal!"

"Go to the pope," I said. "Just get the h--- out of here."

My brother Mike, who was in the tavern with me, thought firing Rose was a bad idea. Of course, looking back, he was right.

"Are you crazy? You're not even supposed to be in here and you fire her? Dad liked her."

"I don't give a d--- who he liked. He wanted me to take care of the place, didn't he?"

Well, as fate would have it, my father got in an accident while he was away. When he returned, Mike urged me not to tell him because he figured dad would be in a terrible mood. But I did anyway.

"I fired Rose," I said. "She gave me some crap and wouldn't take care of the place and clean it."

My father didn't answer.

"Boy, are you lucky," Mike said, once my father was out of earshot.

I turned to him and shook my head. "Are you naive? He's waiting for me. A couple days from now, when I am least expecting it, he's going to attack me on something just to put me in my place."

"Leo, why do you have to fight him?"

"I'm not fighting him, Mike. I'm trying to live to the principles he's disciplined me to have. That's all."

But the reality of what was happening was so much different than I let on. While my father was imprinting his principles on me and telling everyone who would listen that "Leo's just like me," inside I was appalled at the suggestion. I was angry with him for forcing me to quit sports to work at the tavern. And I was angry with him for making me do things his way.

"I'm nothing like you," I told him bitterly, every chance I had.

But my father saw bigger and better things for me—and I never quite understood this while it was happening. As he saw me easily chatting with different kinds of people, he decided that my brother Mike would be channeled into business and I would go into the law. This became his overriding ambition for me. And, while he looked the part of a lawyer with his suit and confident manner, I would be the lawyer, with my confident manner. There is little doubt that my father was the driving force that made me into the influential lawyer he wanted to be. It's a shame I didn't realize what was happening at the time—maybe I'd have acknowledged it a little sooner.

Despite my disagreements with my dad, he was a man of integrity, loyalty and above all, hard work. In his lifetime he developed friendships with President Harry Truman, Vice President Alben Barkley and Sen. Frank Lausche, who became governor of Ohio. Once, he took Lausche to the B.R. Baker clothing store and said, "You're going to be governor now, but you look like a bum. Here are two suits." Can you imagine a former bootlegger telling him that? But they all respected him. This didn't go unnoticed by me.

My father also helped a number of young men attend the U.S. Military Academy and U.S. Naval Academy, just through his influence with the right people—his legacy of good deeds extends far beyond me. As children, we rarely take time to step back, out of the moment, and look at our parents through the right lens. We get caught up solely in our disagreements or resentments. It isn't until later in life that we gain the wisdom to look back and see the context we missed as immature youths.

Despite my father's connections with those who held significant influence, he never let any of them get him under their thumb. Once, when I was 16 years old, I went with my father to the Theatrical Grill, a headquarters for the infamous Cleveland mobster, Alex "Shondor" Birns.

My father told Birns he didn't want an alliance with him. Dad had the respect of everybody because he wouldn't let organized crime figures come into his tavern and throw around their influence. He could always tell the good guys from the bad: "These are good people, these are bad," he would explain. "These are foreigners trying to make a living at a little card game, like your Uncle George."

This was the neighborhood as my father saw it. And there was no place in it for organized crime or crime bosses. Years later, when my father died, Birns showed up at my father's funeral. He drove his big yellow Cadillac convertible in the funeral procession and tried to earn credibility with the locals so that he could make a move on the territory. He was trying to show he was a friend of my dad, but he wasn't. If my father were alive at that time, he would have grabbed Birns and thrown him against the wall.

Even with all of my father's rules and discipline, Mill Tavern could be a dangerous place. It surely was for me—even when it wasn't open yet for the day. On Sundays, when everybody was in church, I would wear plastic gloves and clean around the bar stools where patrons had emptied their full bladders and stuck gum all over the place. I had to scrape it away and clean off the soot and graphite the customers carried in from the steel mill. In my father's bar, you could eat off the floor because he made me clean it so thoroughly.

My father worked his tail off, and he expected—no, demanded—that I follow suit. I didn't understand all this and never quite reconciled how I was expected to do as he ordered. Worse, over the years I had several near-death incidents while tending bar and that made me resent my father for making me work there and exposing me to so much violence.

Some of the altercations happened at Freddie's Bar, one of my father's taverns that was located just down the block from Mill Tavern. Freddie's was operated by my brother Mike, and our father wanted me to help him out. Like a good son, I obeyed and tended bar for the rough crowd that frequented it—putting my life in danger more times than I'd like to remember.

Several other incidents happened at Mill Tavern—drunken fights with switchblades, hammers, knives and broken bottles. Some were more memorable than others. These brushes with death led to countless confrontations with my father, which would almost always go the same way.

"Take this d--- place!" I would yell. "You're making an animal out of me! I hate you!"

"I'm trying to make a man out of you!" he would reply.

"Or get me killed!"

One of the most memorable incidents happened when I was home from college one summer. I was about 19 or 20 years old, and helping my brother Mike at Freddie's Bar. My dad had bought me a $500 Hart Schaffner Marx suit, which I was wearing at the tavern. I told my brother he should call me if there was trouble.

I went behind the bar and sat down to read a magazine. Suddenly, somebody shouted, "Help! Someone is fighting with your brother!"

Mike was in the lounge next door, which was separated from the bar by a door and small hallway.

I ran and grabbed the perpetrator, who was a steelworker and was really strong. I punched him, but he didn't flinch. He laughed at me and tore my suit apart, then threw me over a table.

Just then my friend, Patrolman Johnny Kochan, arrived. He trained my brother and me in the art of self-defense. Years later, I would defend him in a much-celebrated civil rights case. Kochan was a tough Russian who fought professional boxer and Light Heavyweight Champion of the World, Joey Maxim.

While I screamed at the steelworker to move his a--, Kochan just walked up to the steelworker, gave him a short six-inch punch to his jaw, and knocked him out.

This seemingly never-ending stream of danger that was my father's bars wore on me for years, and when I left for college it was as though a weight had been lifted from my shoulders. A strong desire to avoid that violence led to a different kind of decision a few years later, while I was in law school.

Leo's Lesson Learned:

You learn how to deal with all types of people, and it will help you throughout life. You also respect them, and of course, your father.

CHAPTER 6
College

S ome people have warm and cheery memories of going off to college. Mine were a little different. I was an average student, so Ohio University seemed like a good fit, and my brother Mike went there for a year before entering the Air Force.

On the day I headed off to OU, I went to say goodbye to my father.

"Put out your hands," he commanded in Arabic.

I did as he said, thinking he was going to give me money.

Instead, he told me to turn them over.

"If you lie, cheat or steal, I'll cripple you," he said.

I was dumbfounded. Here I was, an 18-year-old kid following my parents' mantra to get an education, and my dad was threatening me for doing things that he ought to have known I wouldn't do.

Today, more than a half-century later, I can readily understand his concerns and his drastic threat. He knew I was an honest kid. I'd always lived by his simple code: Be honest, work hard and you'll have nothing to worry about. But this was his way of warning me against getting contaminated by this new world I'd be entering—a world in which he would no longer be able to protect and control me. My father just didn't have the language to tenderly convey what he felt. All he knew, from early in life, was how to scrape for a living under the brutality of the Ottoman Empire. And so, when he had something important to say, something crucial for his son to understand, he naturally reverted to violent images of eye-for-an-eye justice.

Yet, for all his understandable immigrant fears of new people and new ways, my father could also be quite modern in his attitudes. After all, he was a true Lebanese, a product of an ancient crossroads culture used to entertaining all manner of visitors—friendly or otherwise. For example, he visited my sister in college and told her she could smoke if she wanted (some of her friends were and he wanted her to be modern like them).

Fred got along with people his entire life, but he wasn't compassionate with us and he wasn't compassionate with people he deemed to be idiots. He couldn't tolerate stupidity, but he could have compassion for the people who couldn't have it for themselves. This was at the very essence of his success as a saloonkeeper and as a behind-the-scenes politician in a town where the Lebanese were only a tiny ethnic minority. As a child, he had even figured out how to coexist with the brutal Turkish occupiers. But now, as his son went off to college for the first time, he wanted him to fit in with what he would call the "American people," armed with one last bit of crucial Old World advice.

After acclimating to campus life, the pressure mounted to be accepted and make the grade. I didn't like the feeling of being black-balled from a fraternity because the frat brothers called me a foreigner and thought I was uncouth with my rough-and-tough talk. Further, I wasn't allowed to date women because my father thought they would interfere with my educational goals.

This was the incredible influence my father had on me. He took me like putty and molded me into what he wanted. That's how much I respected him. And that's why he loved me more than everybody else—something I figured out much later in life. To this day, his influence still guides me and the decisions I make.

In many ways, I was a product of the ghetto—Lorain was a hard place, and I learned my vocabulary by listening to prostitutes and tough-guy immigrants who barked out orders in a saloon. It was a freshman speech teacher, Miss Koepps, who would see in me something few other people did. She was only eight years older than me, but had the wisdom and patience of a person three times her age. Miss Koepps' kindness and acute understanding of my personal shortcomings would change everything.

I was a poor candidate for perfect elocution when my personal scenery shifted from Lorain to a peaceful college town in rural southern Ohio. Maybe the change was too severe, or maybe I just had too much independence too quickly, but as my freshman year began I quickly became a listless student. Things were going downhill fast—I was getting a D in speech class—and I was starting to fear telling my father about my situation.

One day, Miss Koepps said she wanted to see me after class.

"What for?" I asked, a touch of attitude in my voice. Defiant, as always.

"I want to talk to you," was all she said.

After the rest of the class left, I demanded anew, "What did I do?"

"Nothing," she said.

"Then why am I here?"

"I'm here to help you learn how to speak," she said. It was an answer that struck me right in the heart.

"I know how to talk," I said, aroused by an old anger that began to well up inside me.

"There's a difference between talking and being a speaker," she said. "I see the potential in you to be a good speaker."

Miss Koepps then proceeded to tick off a list of books I might borrow from the library—books on English composition; and books about famous orators such as William Jennings Bryan and Winston Churchill.

"Read about leaders and how they spoke," she suggested.

"I can't talk like that," I said, still somewhat stunned.

"Whether you can or not, it's important in your education. The tools are speech and writing. That's why I want you to take these books. You'll have an easier time in college. You're a diamond in the rough."

Diamond in the rough. This was a comment that removed a little of the sting from her words and thawed my icy resistance. What she was recommending was a radical departure for me. All my life, I had been motivated out of anger. Anger at the world for throwing me a curveball I couldn't hit. Anger over my father having been sent to prison. Anger just for the sake of being angry. But in her uniquely gentle-but-firm way, Miss Koepps opened another possibility for my life. For the first time, someone motivated me out of the far more powerful emotion than anger: kindness. And it was leaving its mark.

I took Miss Koepps up on her recommendations and began to read about the various great orators in history. As I did, their words began to cast a spell over me. I stumbled across a book of ancient Persian poetry, "The Rubaiyat of Omar Khayyam," and the passage about a jug of wine under a tree reminded me of the love between my grandfather and me. There was another passage in that book that hit me even harder, which spoke directly to me about the pointlessness of my baked-on bitterness:

The Moving Finger writes; and, having writ,
Moves on: nor all thy Piety nor Wit
Shall lure it back to cancel half a Line,
Nor all thy Tears wash out a Word of it.

This was a revelation. I began to understand I couldn't live in the past. I recognized I couldn't dwell on bitterness about my dad's boot-legging. I couldn't focus on my father's prison sentence or my being rejected in certain social circles. No. I had to reject all that and be myself. I had to approach life with a positive outlook and stop worrying about what others thought. In the coming years, illuminating passages of literature such as this helped me focus as never before. It would still take years to fight the demons of the past that were so deeply ingrained in my life, but this was a good start. And decades before I became a Christian, it was as if the Lord began speaking to me through his literary oracles' words, including the message of Philippians 3:13 in the Bible and "forgetting those things which are behind, and reaching forth unto those things which are before." I was beginning to listen.

One fine spring day, my favorite teacher invited me to join her on a picnic. She took along a picnic basket and a blanket. We had a splendid time. And then she did something I'll never forget: She kissed me on the cheek. Just once, and quite chastely. I think she was trying to tell me that I could do it, that I could overcome my handicaps and become someone. In any event, it worked. With her encouragement, I became an increasingly confident person. While I wasn't getting all A's, I was doing good enough work in the classroom to see a real difference in my grades.

However, there were still some on-campus concerns. After the blackballing incident, I went home. I was really upset and disappointed. Thinking how my father fought discrimination and everything that went along with it, I saw my dad's copy of Dale Carnegie's

"How to Win Friends and Influence People" and began reading it. There were chapters like How to Get People to Like You Instantly and The Big Secret of Dealing with People. Those were of great interest to me, and for months I read that book over and over.

When I went back to school for my second year, I applied some of Carnegie's principles. I started to get to know some of the 5,500 students, and knew several hundred by name because of Carnegie's techniques. And so in my sophomore year I decided to pledge another fraternity.

It was around this time that my personality began to take shape. Like my father before me, I had learned Carnegie's core lessons: People are mostly lonely. They respond to those who go out of their way to reach out to them. Somebody has to break the ice. The person who does assumes great power.

Of course, it didn't hurt that I was naturally gregarious and could mix easily with people. I had learned from years of chatting up all kinds of characters in my father's saloon that when you meet people on their conversational turf, they will almost certainly open up to you with enthusiasm. I began using this ability in campus politics. I ran for interfraternity council and nearly unseated an upperclassman incumbent. I also very cautiously dated a few women students. I was still battling my father because I couldn't have a relationship with any girl.

Despite this, my discipline was giving me character. I still didn't have honor roll grades—I earned about a 2.4 average—but was doing much better. My father taught me to stay away from dummies. He said to be polite and try to spend as much time as possible with smart people, especially those smarter than you. This way, you knew your limitations. You learned from them. And they became associates. In his own way he was telling me to be humble and have humility—even if I didn't realize the core principles of his message.

I did take some chances that could have ruined my character—but luckily, none of them did.

The degree I was pursuing, a bachelor's of commerce, required a class in business law. The course was taught by my adviser, Gerald Oliver Dykstra. He was a lawyer and a very bright man. But he was very bitter. I remember him as short, bald and gray. He smoked a pipe and never smiled.

Dykstra looked at me one day and laughed, "You want to be a lawyer? If you want to be a lawyer, you'll be lucky if you graduate from here."

I never forgot that. He didn't think I should have been there. It wasn't even a challenge because you can tell when somebody challenges you. He just flat out had no confidence in me.

Dykstra would come to class and announce himself: "I'm Gerald Oliver Dykstra, G-O-D, God."

That set the stage of what we could expect.

I studied like mad because I knew he had it in for me. It was instinctual—my father passed it along through his DNA. I knew this guy was going to try to flunk me, even though I should have received a B or an A in his class because I had pushed everything else aside to focus on it. Dykstra gave me a D. This was disappointing because I needed at least a C in his class to fulfill my major.

After receiving my grade I went to his house to confront him. When I arrived, he was pulling his car out of the driveway. His wife was sitting next to him. She also taught a law class that I had completed, and I think she liked me.

I went up to his car and said, "You know, Mr. Dykstra, I feel sorry for you."

He looked at me with puzzlement in his face. "What do you want? I don't want to hear anything."

"Look," I said. "I studied hard for your course. I know you've got it in for me. I know I got an A or a B, and you want to stop me with this D, so you don't want me to graduate."

That's when my anger bubbled to the surface, and I grabbed him by his shirt. I was going to belt him. Remember, I was raised in South Lorain and knew little about proper etiquette. Instead, I knew how to survive on the streets.

His wife intervened.

"Leo, Leo," she said. "Leave him alone. I'll talk to him."

I said, "He's not worth it, honey." And I walked away. As I did, I said to myself, "Well, I just got thrown out of school."

Later that day, I received a call from Dykstra's wife.

"Leo, I got him to change it to a C."

"I'd like to apologize," I said.

"That's not necessary. I understand the pressure you're under."

I said, "I love you for what you did for me. Thank you."

She liked me, knew that I appreciated her and that I was really an honest gentleman. I never told too many people about what had happened. If things had gone the other direction my whole career would have been over right there. After this incident, I changed and became a more dedicated student. But I still had a ways to go before I learned how to be humble.

Four months before my graduation from college, my father took me to the Dodge dealer to show me what he was going to get me for graduation. This was his grand gesture, the way he was going to show his love. Earlier, he had bought my brother a Dodge coupe, so to me this seemed like more a way to appease me than to reward me. So what did I do? I told him, "I don't want it."

My father looked at me and said, "You ungrateful little s---."

He didn't show any emotion, and I didn't give a d---.

"I can get my own car," I said.

"What kind of car do you want?" my father asked.

"Never mind, I'll get my own," I replied. "I'm going to get myself a Rocket 88 Oldsmobile." That was the hottest car around, and I wanted one.

I returned to school and came back home again about a month before graduation. My grandmother, my mother, my father and I were having dinner together.

After dinner, my father pulled me aside.

"I want to talk to you," he said.

"Geez, here goes another lecture."

"Just follow me."

So I followed my father outside and there, to my surprise, was the Rocket 88.

That's when I knew my father loved me. It was a defining moment in our relationship. I still cry today whenever I retell the story.

My grandmother said, "You should worship that man." And while she was afraid of him as her son, she saw his goodness, kindness and tenderness. He didn't want to show weakness. His demeanor was a blend of bitterness and strength.

Whether my father was trying to clarify his relationship with me in what would become his final months, nobody can say. But I received a second compliment shortly after that. My cousin, George Koury Jr., son of my Uncle George and Aunt Zana—who had tried to have a child for 14 years—was born. My father declined Uncle George's request that he be godfather, deferring the honor to me. This was the second compliment he gave me.

My aunt and uncle had a picture taken of me holding my new god-son in my arms and then baptizing him. My father made a statement I'll never forget: "I wish I was you, Leo."

Looking at the photo, I can't help but notice how my father looked admiringly at me. I was 21 with wavy hair and the temporary slim good looks of youth. Unlike my father, I had been well-educated. I was headed for law school and almost visibly confident in my future. And, my father had said five magic words: "I wish I was you."

At the time, I wondered why he had said it. It was the first time he had complimented me, and I saw it as approval. I thought he was so smart for a guy who came from the old country, who had the respect of presidents, senators and everybody else. He had bootlegged for survival, not because he was a criminal.

I almost cry when I think about it now, how my father missed out on other opportunities in life. Why was I so blessed? For years this tormented me. But it also motivated me to succeed. As the old Lebanese saying goes, "Honor thy father." In Arabic, I would say, "Hatha ibn Fuad Khouri:" This is the son of Fred Koury.

By doing so, you perpetuate his name, memory and everything through you. I never understood that until later. I owe it all to him and God, but I didn't realize I loved my father that much until later.

Leo's Lesson Learned:
Let nothing stop you in your efforts to get an education and become a lawyer. It is my vision for you, and you must follow it. And while I might not say it, I do love you.

CHAPTER 7

Law School and Sadness

I enrolled at the University of Cincinnati College of Law, the fourth oldest continually running law school in the United States. After six weeks of classes, I found myself with serious doubts about whether I'd make it through the program.

On the first day of school, Dean Frank Rowley addressed the new students with this sobering prediction: "Look to your left, look to your right. One of you three will not be here to graduate."

So I looked to my left and then my right, and suddenly thought he was talking about me. It was a sobering thought, one that turned into a real crisis when I got a C on Dean Rowley's first contracts course exam. I went into the dean's office after receiving my grade with the intention of discussing my concerns.

"What's the matter?" he asked.

"I don't think I'm suited to be a lawyer," I said. "I studied really hard, and I remember what you said, 'One of the three will not be here.' I must not have known the material well."

Dean Rowley looked at me, quietly, and then said, "Son, the A and B students will become teachers or big corporate lawyers. You will be a good trial lawyer."

I didn't know how to take that, so I called my father and said, "Dad, I think I want to come home."

It was the first time he didn't raise his voice when I offered up something potentially controversial.

"Son, what's the problem?"

"Law school is too tough," I said. "There are 110 people in our class and the dean says one out of every three of us are not going to make it."

It was a hard conversation for me to have with my father—letting him see the doubt in my mind. But I had the guts to say this because I was 260 miles away from him; I would have never worked up the courage to say it to his face.

My father's response took me by surprise.

"Son," he said. "If it was easy, everyone would be there."

I'll never forget that. And then my father said, "Be patient. You're going to be somebody."

I think he sort of lied at that point. How would he know if I were going to be anybody? But when he said that, it gave me the encouragement I needed. And I was able to make it through that first year of law school.

Feeling confident that I was opening a new chapter in my life, I decided to work somewhere other than my father's saloons. This was the first time in my life I did something independent. I went to U.S. Steel and told Mr. Reese, who was a friend of my father, "Give me the dirtiest job but don't tell my dad."

He hired me to grease the machinery, and it probably was the worst and dirtiest job they had. But I didn't complain. I was there about a month when my father said to me, "Why are you embarrassing me?"

"Embarrassing you?" I replied. "How am I embarrassing you?"

"My son…working in there," he said.

"It's an honest job, Dad," I said, and looked him right in the eye and continued. "Do you want me to be a saloonkeeper or do you want me to be a lawyer? I need time to study and read books. I don't have time to put up with drunks at this stage of my life."

My father started to say something in reply, but thought better of it and kept his mouth shut. I was surprised—but happy—that he backed down.

One month later, I was working in the machinery pits, covered in dirt and grease, when someone let me know I had an important phone call. It was the bar manager. My father, he said, had a heart attack.

"Come to St. Joseph's Hospital as fast as you can."

I raced over there.

When I arrived, my father was in bed. I gave him a kiss, and asked him where the keys were for the bar.

"I'm going to take it over," I said. "I'm quitting my job, and I want you to get well; I'm going to go get the keys."

Then I left my father, went home to change, and settled in to attend to whatever affairs I could while my father was laid up. But soon after, I received another phone call.

"You had better get back to the hospital."

I rushed back to the hospital and went back to my dad's bedside. But I was too late. He had died while I was on my way. I kissed him again and said, "I'm sorry. I'm sorry that I didn't…" I guess I was going to apologize for failing him.

My father was 47 years old. I buried him on my 23rd birthday.

If there were any doubts about my father's status in the community, they were forever erased by the throngs of people that turned out for his funeral. They came from across the state of Ohio and far beyond—all of them there to pay their respects. In a fitting bit of irony, the parking lot of the local newspaper, the Lorain Journal, which for years had personally attacked my father as a racketeer, was rendered impassable for hours because of all the mourners' cars.

(As an aside here, my father told me: "Do not answer a newspaper. The reason is that they have the last word. They only care for sensation and they'll go up in the highest building and wait for you to walk and drop a bucket of manure on you." I never answered requests for interviews or comments from newspapers for many years, even as I would be rammed left and right later in life. But things turned around when the Lorain Journal publisher Harry Horvitz apologized for his newspaper's criticism of me—and offered me the olive branch of a partnership in a Lorain County cable television venture he was forming that would take some representation before the FCC.)

The funeral service was held at the Church of the Redeemer, which had more seating than the Orthodox church where my father belonged. It was four hours long. A dinner for 300 guests in the American Legion Hall followed. Speakers at the dinner included Mayor Patrick J. Flaherty, State Rep. Leslie Burge, City Prosecutor Raymond Miraldi, Ohio State Employee Service Lorain Office Manager Ward A. Riley, former Assistant U.S. District Attorney Howell Leuck and attorney Joseph Saslow of Cleveland. The theme of this procession of speakers was, as the Lorain Journal reported, to laud my father's accomplishments: "Fred Koury was a man of high quality and widespread ambition. He was very successful in all his endeavors and ranked high in the community."

To my brother Mike and me, the speakers said, "It would only be fitting and proper that as sons of Fred Koury that you would mold your life in the same channel in which your father attained such high goals."

Another news account said my father was known to be one of the most powerful behind-the-scenes political leaders in the history of Lorain.

It took 10 pallbearers to carry the 1,000-pound copper casket into the church. These included Ward A. Riley, James Gedling, Edmond Hanna, Fred Karem, Louie Fadel, Offie Mallo, John Elias, John Simon, Assad Abraham and Frank Tegreene.

Many people came to my father's funeral, but I was so bitter about the loss that I really couldn't talk to any of them. Despite our differences, my father was always the compass in my life. Without him, I suddenly found myself at a crossroads: Should I run his business and take care of the family or should I become the lawyer he wanted me to be?

What would my father want me to do? If he really loved me, and if I really believed it, how would that realization play itself out? At the time, I honestly didn't know.

It took a fateful visit by mourner Tony Marquez to help me find the answers I was seeking. Tony was a regular at Mill Tavern. He was a bachelor, and my father rented a room above the business to him. Tony would arrive at the bar from work covered in graphite. He would get loaded on beer, sit in a booth and wouldn't bother anyone. My dad would say, "Watch over him. Don't let anybody bother him or try to shake money or anything from him." In fact, my father wouldn't let him keep his money with him; he'd either hold his money or give Tony credit. My father treated him like a wayward child. That was my dad—tender...without ever really showing it.

We were at the funeral home when Tony asked to see me. I had been stone-faced and standoffish up until then. People would come up and offer their condolences, and I would just nod.

"Sure," I said. "Send him over."

Tony came up to me slowly but confidently. He knelt down at the kneeling rail, said a prayer, and then started crying.

"He loved me," he cried. "He loved me!"

That's when I knew my father couldn't show love, except through his actions—the way he did things. He could never bring himself to say the words. But in that one moment, when Tony cried, I really understood just how much my father loved me, and that he had spent his life showing me without actually telling me. And that was when I said to myself, "I'm going to be that lawyer."

My mission was clear. I quit my steel mill job and went to work with my brother Mike running my father's bars for the rest of the summer. Once it was time to return to law school Mike assumed the leadership role. I am beholden to my brother because he wouldn't let me quit after my father died. He took care of my mother for two years so I could finish law school. Then he did it for two more years when I served in the Army, even sending my sister Joan to college so she could become a teacher. My brother Mike stepped up to the plate when he needed to, and I am forever grateful.

While I was finishing law school, I received my induction notice from the Selective Service System, telling me I was about to be drafted into the U.S. Army during the Korean War. I had received deferments when I was an undergraduate student, but my last deferment was set to expire before I was done with law school.

As it turns out, a Lorain dentist who was head of the local draft board blamed my father for instituting a gambling raid on the American Legion Hall. He said that Fred Koury held power with the liquor department and sent the authorities for the raid. My father said he never did that, and would never call in a raid. But the dentist decided he made a good scapegoat and implicated him. Because of this, they came after me while I was still in law school and issued orders for induction.

But that wasn't the end of it. Burge, who was a friend of my dad's, got wind of the situation and went to bat for me with the draft board. Burge was able to get the board to extend my deferment until after I graduated. Sure enough, my induction order arrived shortly after graduation. And wouldn't you know it, that son-of-a-gun dentist was right there to make sure I got on the bus.

My brother Mike, who had served in World War II and had bouts of post-traumatic stress disorder afterward, saw me off. As we said our goodbyes, Mike started crying.

"Why are you crying?" I asked.

"Because you're going off to be killed," he said.

"You were in combat," I said, trying to console him. "Your crew members were killed but you survived. This is the end of the Korean War. I'll be fine. And then I'll be back home."

That wasn't good enough. My brother just stood there and cried his heart out as I boarded the bus. He was sure I was going to die.

I was assigned to Fort Knox, Kentucky, for basic training. Because I was rushed off to the Army so soon after graduation I still didn't know the results of the bar exam I had taken. Six weeks in, I was called to regimental headquarters.

As I walked into the office, I was wondering whether I had done something wrong or if there was a problem with my family back home.

A lieutenant handed me a slip of paper.

"Sign this," he said.

"What is it?"

"An emergency pass," he said.

I didn't understand. "What is it for?"

"Don't ask questions, soldier. Just sign it and get out."

So I signed the pass and packed up to leave. I tried to call my mother, whom I thought might be sick. She had terrible asthma, and I thought she might have had an attack…or worse, a heart attack. I finally reached my Aunt Zana, who told me my mother was fine. "Everything's alright," she said. "Congratulations, Leo. You passed the bar exam!"

The pass was so that I could travel to Cincinnati to be sworn in with the rest of my class as an official lawyer. It was an interesting trip because before the Army, I had beautiful, wavy hair. Now, my head was shaved and I wore a buck privates uniform. All the guys were laughing like hell when I was being sworn in. But it was worth it. I was an official lawyer now—just like my father had always wanted me to be.

When I got back to Fort Knox, my presence was requested once more at the regimental headquarters. There, I was offered the opportunity to become a first lieutenant and judge advocate general, which meant an officer and a lawyer practicing for the U.S. Army.

"What's the commitment?" I asked.

"Three years."

That wouldn't fly. I explained that my mother was a widow and wasn't well. I just couldn't do that to her.

"What other options are there for an attorney without having to become a judge advocate general," I asked.

"You could serve as a Troop Information and Education instructor."

It would come with all the benefits and privileges of an officer without the rank. That sounded good, so I was shipped off to military intelligence school in New York where they would teach me how to serve as a defense against the brainwashing the enemy was doing in Korea. My job would be to read a lot. So I read daily newspapers, *Time* magazine, American history books and publications devoted to democracy. I also read about current events. Then I would talk to U.S. servicemen about America and ensure they weren't being brainwashed against our country. It was certainly an easier way to spend my time than preparing to go to war.

Twenty-two months later, the Korean War ended. My time in the military was over, and I headed back home to Ohio.

Leo's Lesson Learned:
Be honest, be honorable, do your time and get out.
Don't make a career of the military if you're not cut out to be a
military man. If you're meant to be a lawyer, be a lawyer.

My parents, Fred and Mary Koury's wedding photo, circa 1924. Notice the fountain pen in my dad's pocket, ready to sign paperwork. His best man was a friend of his and the maid of honor was Elizabeth Dave, one of my mother's cousins.

Fred Koury, circa 1930. Always nattily attired, my dad knew quality clothing. That's probably a Cuban cigar in his hand.

Our first family photo, circa 1934: Fred and Mary Koury, with Michael, Joan and me. I'm wearing short pants, and I am perfecting my ornery look.

A few years later, I was glad to show how dear my sister Joan was to me.

My brother Mike and I in front of Mill Tavern, the bar was both the breadwinner and bane of my existence. Mike had just returned from serving as an aerial gunner in the Eighth Air Force over Germany in World War II.

My grandfather, Isaac Koury, who spoiled me rotten, in front of his house on East 30th Street in Lorain, circa 1930s.

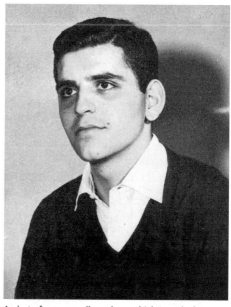

A photo from my college days, which I used when I was running for interfraternity council.

In the mid-1950s, Lila and her father John Rashid, left, went to Lebanon, where on a lark, Lila was entered in a Miss Lebanon competition and won. At a reception, she met President Camille Chamoun, who led the country from 1952 to 1958.

Lila and I in 1958, at the time of our wedding. I remember spending all my money on our honeymoon to Nassau.

This family photo was taken a short time before my mother Mary passed away in 1989 at the age of 85. My sister Joan, her daughter Claudia and I are in the back row and my mother and brother Mike are in the front.

One of my favorite recent photos of Lila and me.

My sister Joan with her husband Charlie Haddad.

A celebratory photo taken after victory in the Kochan case. From left to right, Patrolman Johnny Kochan, Sgt. Richard Griffith, myself and Maxwell Gruber.

Two Lorain policemen and their lawyers at their trial in U.S. District Court yesterday. Left to right are Maxwell J. Gruber, Sgt. Richard L. Griffith, E. G. (Leo) Koury, and Patrolman John F. Kochan.

Plain Dealer Photo (Dudley Brumbach)

Police Beat Morales Brutally, Jury Is Told

★ From First Page

little too much beer, McCurdy said, and scuffled with the man who drove the ther car and with police who ame to quiet the fray. Morales was taken to the Lorain 'olice Station, locked in a ell and charged with disturbng the peace and resisting rrest.

At 10 p.m. on Jan. 13—24 ours after he had been incarcerated, McCurdy said, gt. Griffith and Patrolman ochan took Morales to an terrogation room. There, IcCurdy said Morales was aten when he refused to dless to any narcotic ofnses.

Griffith and Kochan were en the two-man vice squad the Lorain Police Department.

GRIFFITH knocked Morales f a chair with a blow from blackjack, McCurdy said.

four policemen to subdue Morales, Gruber said, when he was taken from a vice squad car and put into a "paddy wagon." The policemen, Gruber said, had to beat Morales into submission.

The next night, Gruber said, Griffith and Kochan were assigned to investigate a report that Morales' condition the night before had been caused by narcotics rather than alcohol.

The questioning of Morales by the two policemen was not accompanied by brutality, Gruber said, but Morales refused to cooperate in any way. One of the trips to the interrogation room, Gruber said, was at Morales' request which he sent to Griffith and Kochan through a turnkey on the cell block.

GRUBER SAID Morales was the leader of a terrorist gang made up of pachucos.

or ruffians. The gang u tattoo marks on their ha and arms for identificati Gruber said he would sh that Morales' arm bore " chevron of the gang leade

Gruber described the se men who wrote the descr tion of Morales' wounds m paper bag as hoodlums of it standing who were trying get even with the police. said some were members Morales' gang.

Morales will be the first v ness.

Angelo Morales

A 1965 clipping from The Plain Dealer when I defended Patrolman Johnny Kochan.

Another celebratory photo, taken after I won back union official Carl Roberts' job with the local steelworkers' union.

The Koury Building in Lorain, built over the ashes of Mill Tavern on Pearl Avenue.

I commissioned this oil painting of myself, which really communicates my no-nonsense demeanor.

"Someday, God willing, we are going to beat the odds and make childhood cancer a thing of the past," Danny Thomas said. Here I am giving him a $2,500 check from an ALSAC fundraiser to build St. Jude Children's Research Hospital in Memphis.

I told Christine Gitlin, "Bring Jimmy Carter to Lorain, Ohio, and I'll raise a thousand dollars." Well, he came, and we shook hands among all the politicos.

Ever personable, Jimmy Carter was great at photo ops.

President Jimmy Carter always obliged for a photo. This was at a White House reception. Lila was impressed with his character.

Carter signed this photo of the famous handshake between himself, Anwar Sadat of Egypt and Menachem Begin of Israel.

At a White House dinner, I met Ezer Weizman, then Israeli minister of defense (he later became president of Israel). He asked me if I was going to the meeting at Camp David, and I said, "No. They didn't invite me to that one. I'm too outspoken." He said, "That's a shame. You'd be great." I said, "Well, I heard you're great, too. Because you're objective." He invited me to Israel; I thanked him and said, "When there is peace in Lebanon, I'd be honored to visit."

After I stopped rubbing elbows with politicos, I spent time on other friendships, such as with famed Los Angeles Dodgers manager Tommy Lasorda. Patsie Campana loaned us his private jet to take Lasorda to Atlantic City to meet Donald Trump. Tagging along were Patsie's son Bob Campana and grandson Anthony Campana, and Joseph Coury, founder of PharMed.

My best friend was Pasquale "Patsie" Campana Sr., founder of the P.C. Campana Co. We had first met on a school playground when he protected me as I was being bullied. Later, we parted for a while but then rekindled our friendship, which lasted for many years.

My wife, Lila (center), with John Murtha and his wife Marie. John lead Bible study at Joe and Jeanette Kanaan's home.

"I, Billy Graham, am a sinner. All of us are sinners."

The Billy Graham Crusade in June 1994 marked the beginning of my redemption through salvation. It was held at the Cleveland Municipal Stadium.

Joe and Jeanette Kanaan, owners of Joe's Restaurant, to whom I owe gratitude for urging me forward on my journey to accept Christ, especially with the Bible study at their home. Jeannette also ushered me to TV reporter Lorrie Taylor at the Billy Graham Crusade.

Our pilgrimage to the Billy Graham Library included my son-in-law Anthony Valore, my sons Lee and Fred, myself, Anthony Campana and his father Bob Campana (Patsie Campana's son).

My visit to Koubba was time to make new acquaintances with relatives.

Lila's brother Dr. Floyd Rashid, a dentist, and Mae Rashid, mother to Lila and Floyd, who is a centenarian and still going strong.

This is the house where my father lived in Koubba. It is now occupied by relatives of our family, the El-Royheb clan.

Our Koubba relatives hosted a reception for us with former President Émile Lahoud. Most were too young to have known my father, but knew of his reputation and his generous gifts to the local church throughout his life. Standing are Jenelle and Floyd Rashid, Samira Hussney, President Lahoud, Father André of St. George Antiochian Orthodox Church in Koubba, Lila and me.

Lila and I with our four wonderful children: Lee, Janet, Fred and Lisa.

Lila and me with our eldest daughter's family. Standing are Brian Yurovich and his wife Jennifer, our granddaughter; Corey and her husband Richard, our grandson; our daughter Lisa and her husband Jim Faro. Seated are Lila, me and our granddaughter Stephanie.

Our son Fred, his wife Lena and their sons Michael and Joey.

Janet, our daughter, and her husband Anthony Valore.

Our son Lee, his wife Gretchen and their children, Eli, Halle, Annie and Lila.

CHAPTER 8

Arriving

In 1955, I returned home to Lorain. I was officially a lawyer. Life was about to become grand. Well, at least that's what I thought. But that silly notion soon faded away when I started hunting for a position. I went down all the usual routes for novice attorneys—friends, acquaintances, public officials. What irked me was again being called the son of a bootlegger. It definitely bothered me back then to be known as the bootlegger's son.

One prospective employer tried to talk me into going to another city because of the negative connotations of the Koury name. My father's bootlegging past still haunted our family name, as did the reputation of my Uncle George, who was a well-known gambler in the community.

"You know, Leo, it's better if you went elsewhere to practice law," he told me.

It felt like a knife had just been thrust through my heart. I was shocked and hurt. Here I thought this man was my father's friend since dad helped him get his appointment to office. Despite my father's shortcomings, he was well respected. So I just couldn't understand why this was happening.

Thank God for my dad's old friend Joe Ujhelyi. Joe was a prominent lawyer and longtime chairman of the county Democratic Party. Our families went back even further than he and my dad's longtime friendship. His father, who owned a winery, had known my grandfather, Isaac. Joe gave me a small office to use for no rent, and started referring some small cases my way.

For the next few years, I ground it out as a young lawyer, looking to Joe for advice and insight along the way as I developed my craft. I was eternally grateful. As a show of gratitude, my brother Mike—who was by then a real estate broker and World War II hero—Joe, and I formed a real estate partnership called J.E.M. The "J" stood for Joe, the "E" for Elias and the "M" for Michael. We bought an old shopping strip on Pearl Avenue—with the Lorain Theater—and a theater on Grove Avenue called the Grove Theater, and would go on to do some other business together.

Joe helped naturalize a lot of the foreigners who settled in Lorain. He wouldn't charge them, which is how he kept building up a loyal constituency. Joe would offer me advice whenever he could, such as "Leo, never forget this in politics. It's not important who is for you; it's how many."

I respected him and loved him like a surrogate father. I included Joe in every enterprise that my brother and I had in real estate.

By the time we were working together, Joe had become an almost mythic character in Lorain. He was tall and well-built, looked like a big Swede and had two nicknames: You either called him Toughie or Uncle Joe, just like Joseph Stalin.

Joe dominated everything. He ran the party just as toughly as he ran the local booster club for the Cleveland Browns. When he'd place a call, he was known to bark into the phone: "Shut up. This is 'U' talking." He was rougher and tougher than anyone I had ever met. When people called him "ukulele" and teased him about how difficult it was to say his name, he had a typically combative response: "Well, it's hard to say your name in Hungarian."

Before Uncle Joe arrived on the scene as county party chairman, Lorain—both the city and the county—had been heavily Republican. In the mid- to late-1930s, as the Depression set in, Joe started registering ethnic immigrants with a fury. His strength as a lawyer was twofold: he wasn't greedy, and he was intensely loyal. He continued to live in the old neighborhood long after he had become wealthy enough to move to a much grander address.

It took Joe about five years to change the balance of power in Lorain County—tipping the political balance from Republication to Democrat, and attracting the enmity of the former power brokers, banks, utilities and newspapers. They attacked him every way they could. They were the real robber barons, stealing with but a flourish of the pen. But Uncle Joe's specialty was math. He was better at accounting and stockpiling votes than anyone else.

His famous saying, repeated more times than I care to remember, was that, "When I go sober up some poor hunky (Hungarian) and get him to the polls, his vote's just as good as Vanderbilt's or Carne-gie's."

It was true. In politics, it's not who's for you but how many.

These Democrat votes increased in proportion to the number of favors Joe and my father did for people. With every free act of legal work, Joe made a friend. And before long, those friends combined to become a powerful Democrat machine—probably the most power-ful in Ohio in the mid-20th century.

While Joe was tending to the party, someone had to do the legal grunt work on all the penny-ante cases that came his way. Of course, that's where I came in. For example, liquor licenses. The owners and patrons of local clubs and bars formed the backbone of Joe's constit-uency. And Joe never said "No" to any request.

"I'm hungry," I told him. "Can't they at least pay my gas?"

They never did.

"U" wasn't the only one benefiting from my law degree. My brother Mike would refer people with legal problems to me as well. He would say they knew your father or your grandfather. That was code for, "Don't charge them."

I wasn't thrilled about working so hard for so little money, but I was also aware of the great education I was getting in law as well as in politics. Joe's longtime secretary, Rose Skolnicki Dellisanti, for ex-ample, was especially helpful in teaching me some of the finer points of negotiating bureaucracies. That knowledge clearly beat hanging out my shingle alone.

Meanwhile, I was forming my own tough, forbidding shell. This should not have been surprising to anyone, especially considering that my two primary role models were my father and Joe. And, I was forever conscious of the fact that I had to work 10 times as hard as other young lawyers whose fathers or grandfathers were attorneys or judges. As a result, I developed a chip on my shoulder. Whenever someone got in my way I threatened to belt them. If I wouldn't be accepted and invited to practice my profession in my hometown, I'd force it. My behavior back then wasn't very Christian-like, but then again, neither was I.

During my grunt-work years, I gave a lot of legal aid to those less fortunate than others in society. I didn't have an inkling that things could be different. An assistant prosecutor once scolded me about one of my pro bono clients: "You're going to ruin your career, representing a guy like that."

I didn't have much patience for that kind of reasoning.

"I don't have a career," I told him. "I'm just trying to make a living."

That was true. As a lawyer, I was getting by, just barely. And then Johnny Kochan got into trouble and changed my life.

It was 1964. I had been practicing law for nearly a decade. Johnny was a Lorain cop, but I had known him earlier as a young guy who had frequented my dad's saloon. He had saved me from a near-death altercation while I was working at Freddie's Bar. Like my Uncle George, he was a boxer. Each had a healthy respect for the other, and I can recall Johnny and Uncle George sizing each other up as though they were preparing to face each other in the ring.

One day, Johnny called me to say he needed a lawyer. He was so matter-of-fact about his situation that I at first thought he was talking about something as routine as a speeding ticket. Little did I know what I was getting into by agreeing to help him out with his problem.

Patrolman Kochan was being charged with one of the most serious violations possible: He and another vice squad member, Lorain Police Sgt. Richard Griffith, were facing charges for allegedly beating a teenage Mexican-American drug suspect, Angelo Morales, with a blackjack in order to extract information about the narcotics trade in Lorain. Because of this beating, the two allegedly secured a false confession from him. As if that weren't bad enough, the two officers' accusers were not members of the county legal system but instead federal prosecutors. The two were being charged under a new federal civil rights statute that made it a crime to discriminate against blacks and other minorities.

This case would become my ticket to enter the big leagues and served as the next critical step in my education as a lawyer. Until that case, my practice had focused exclusively on small issues and I had no trial experience. Besides the slew of liquor law violations for Joe, I worked on such mundane matters as uncontested divorces, personal wills and traffic violations for clients of modest means. At the same time, I knew only too well that I wasn't remotely qualified to try a case in federal court. I would need to team up with a veteran trial lawyer, who could take the lead in presenting the case to a jury after I had helped develop the evidence. That man would be Maxwell Gruber, a friend of my father's. He is the person who really taught me how to be a great lawyer.

I had first met him years before, when my father had taken me to Gruber's Restaurant in Shaker Heights, outside Cleveland, which was owned by his family. He and his brother, Roman, ran the restaurant, which from the late 1940s to late 1950s was one of the most popular establishment for fine dining in Northeast Ohio and acted as a social center for the affluent residential community of Shaker Heights.

The secret to becoming a great trial lawyer is pretty easy, really. All it takes is massive preparation. Both the prosecution and the defense must have such an intimate command of the facts and evidence that they could recite the case in their sleep. This is where Gruber stepped in and taught me what to do.

He also taught me the paramount importance of honesty. Once you lie as a lawyer, he warned, you'll be forever labeled as such and lose your credibility in court. And like my first legal mentor, Joe, Gruber counseled me that money is not the most important thing as a lawyer. Winning should always come first.

Over the years, I was cited by judges for infractions. But they never threw me in jail because I had credibility. They knew I fought for my client. Citations were always a bit political. Judges used them to let people know that Leo Koury—or other lawyers—didn't run their courtrooms.

Gruber also taught me to literally exhaust myself with preparation, to thoroughly brief a case out by digging into the law books and reading everything relevant. He stressed the importance of seeking out the best possible expert witnesses to buttress the case, whatever the cost. When the Fraternal Order of Police raised about $5,000 for the two officers' defense, Gruber knew exactly how to spend it for maximum leverage. He hired a couple of former FBI agents to investigate the evidence. As a hungry young lawyer, that made me wince. But I was hardly in a position to object. Instead, to put bread on the table for my family while I worked on this massive undertaking, I ran back and forth to Lorain to work on smaller cases.

For months, we painstakingly prepared the defense. From the start, I believed Johnny's denials—and not just because he was my friend. The accusation that he had used a blackjack simply didn't ring true. I knew this guy, and something didn't smell right. Johnny's deep professional pride as a boxer would had made him use the most lethal weapons at his disposal—his fists.

Our investment in crack investigators quickly turned into money well spent. Their thoroughness uncovered glaring inconsistencies in the plaintiff's story. Contrary to his testimony, you couldn't hear hollering from his cell to where he said others heard it. More damaging still, we uncovered evidence of a "kangaroo court" in the county jail, in which a group of prisoners had made a pact to falsely accuse the officers as a form of revenge. This was hard to prove but certainly something that we could leverage to our benefit.

In March 1965, the case went to trial in U.S. District Court in Cleveland. This was one of the first civil rights cases to go to trial in America, so naturally there was massive press coverage.

Even armed with good solid defensive evidence we had our work cut out for us. The prosecution team was impressive. It was led by U.S. District Attorney Merle McCurdy, an African-American who had been appointed by former U.S. Attorney General Bobby Kennedy. In his three-and-a-half years on the job, McCurdy had never lost a case. He was a rising star, and there was a lot of speculation that he was in line to be appointed a federal judge.

As impressive a courtroom performer as Gruber was, McCurdy was even better. Gruber was professorial, and I soaked up his lessons. But McCurdy was something altogether different; he was like Hollywood's idealized image of a powerful mid-career attorney. He moved like a panther, and when he quietly framed his arguments for a jury, all eyes were on him. I watched in astonishment, immediately aware that I was in the presence of a master. During the two-week trial, the prosecution had as many as a dozen lawyers taking part, some sitting at the prosecution table, others hurrying in and out of the courtroom delivering various tidbits of research or evidence.

At one point during the trial, as McCurdy was making his point, he dropped a document he was about to enter as an exhibit. I immediately went to pick it up for him, prompting spectators to erupt in laughter. My action was intended to show my humility to the jurors, but in truth I was also more than a little intimidated. McCurdy was so good that at times I felt as though it was me on trial and not my client.

After a grueling 12-day trial, the jury of seven women and five men returned its verdict: The officers were acquitted of all charges.

As the verdict was read, I saw Johnny Kochan cry for the first time. McCurdy's face on the other hand, was ashen. I labored to keep my emotions in check, since Gruber had counseled me beforehand, "Either way it goes, keep your cool."

And, instead of showing emotion in victory, I commended McCurdy on his performance (years later, we became friends). But once we left the courtroom, and I was away from everyone, I finally let out a whoop.

"Wow!" I said, to no one in particular.

In fact, much of Lorain was jubilant.

"Law and order scored a resounding victory..." editorialized the Lorain Journal, which contributed to the defense fund perhaps partly because of the black eye a guilty verdict would give the city but also because the closely watched case was good for its reputation.

In the end, winning trials in federal court would become like a drug for me. Looking back now from a different perspective I realize I lacked humility. Instead, I let the winning create a high for me, not unlike that from opium, and craved more. The publicity received from winning cases in federal court fed my bad habit. It fed my ego, which at the time was too big for my own good. It didn't help that there were fringe benefits. Shortly after the verdict, I was driving near Toledo when I got stopped for speeding. As the patrolman studied my driver's license, his eyebrows raised a little.

"Koury," he mused. "Are you related to the Koury in the federal case?"

When I told him I was the guy, he not only didn't write me a ticket but he gave me an escort to the state line. That did little to tamp down my then-un-Christian-like behavior. But the winning was good for attracting new clients.

Despite the benefits, federal trial work takes too much out of you to be enjoyable—at least for me. Once, I had to be hospitalized for exhaustion. And the time necessary to do it right completely erodes the time you have to see your family. In fact, it's become axiomatic that nearly all superlawyers have terrible family lives, if indeed they have any at all. But I pressed on—because it's what I did—and would proceed to handle numerous interesting cases over the next few years.

One involved Carl Roberts, president of the 7,000-member United Steelworker Union Local 1104 from U.S. Steel Corp.'s Lorain Works. The international union had suspended Roberts for a year for a series of articles he had written that were published in the local's weekly newspaper, the Lorain Labor Leader. The articles supported an opponent of the well-known president of the international union, I.W. Abel.

Gruber and I defended Roberts through the U.S. District Court, which overruled his suspension, and into the U.S. Sixth Circuit Court of Appeals in Cincinnati. We won, and Roberts was granted the right to run for a third term as president. In 1970, he won re-election by 300 votes.

With so many high-profile cases, I realized how tough it would be to go back to being just a small-town lawyer working on nickel-and-dime cases. The Kochan case, followed by a progressive of other high-profile cases vaulted me into a different level of success in my career. From that point forward, no longer would I be forced to sweat a lot for little reward. If my father were looking down on me, he would have been very, very proud.

Leo's Lesson Learned:
Surround yourself with people who are smarter than you and take care of business: TCB.

CHAPTER 9

Lila

My early days as a lawyer in Lorain in the mid-1950s started out slowly, but picked up as the decade progressed. While it wasn't until the mid-1960s when the high-profile cases kicked my career into high gear, 1957 marked a turning point. That's when Lila entered my life—and the world changed.

When we met, I was a 29-year-old lawyer trying to eke out a living. Back then, I was a bachelor and, not surprisingly, dating. Unfortunately for my mother, none of the women were Lebanese.

"Are you ashamed of your people?" she'd ask.

"Not at all," I said. "But Lebanese women, for the most part, just don't appeal to me."

Dark-haired people tend to be attracted to their opposites, and so was I. Blondes and redheads were more along the lines of my taste. But to appease my mother, I promised I'd attend a Syrian Orthodox convention at the Hotel Cleveland, where single Lebanese women from all over the country would be out in full force, chaperoned by their families.

The affair was scheduled to begin at 8 p.m. Saturday, on what was a beautifully sunny summer evening. It was August 17, 1957—a date I'll never forget. As it happened, that day I was with my friend John Dandrea and a couple of dates, sunbathing on his boat. I forgot about the time as it rolled past. Eventually, though, John got me to the hotel, just before midnight.

My mother chastised me for my tardiness. My brother and my uncle were focused on introducing me to an interesting girl from Peoria, Illinois, and went straight to work. I had other ideas, though, and I kept delaying meeting this girl from Peoria.

Finally, however, I got her name and we talked for a little while. She was Roman Catholic; her mother was Syrian Orthodox, like our family, so we had some things in common.

"Why do you come to these conventions?" I asked her.

"Because my mother wants me to," she replied.

Little did I know that her mother—with some divine intervention—would play a bigger part in our saga. I had a short romantic attention span in those days, and I soon left the event. This pretty young girl from Illinois, Lila Rashid, formed a quick impression that I was just one of many guys whom she probably would never see again. God, however, was hard at work behind the scenes.

As the summer ended and Labor Day weekend approached, I didn't think much more about the event or my family's attempt at matchmaking. My friend Archie Delis and I decided to put his convertible to good use for the holiday weekend.

"You know, I met a nice girl from Peoria," I said as we drove around. "You know where that is?"

"Sure do."

"Interested in a road trip?"

"Maybe."

I called Lila and told her we were coming to Peoria. I was bringing a friend, and asked if she could line up a date for him. At first, she didn't have any luck. But then, about a half-hour later, she called back to say she drafted her cousin Emily.

Off we went.

I couldn't believe how far away Peoria turned out to be. We seemed to drive for days—this was in the days before there were superhighways. When we got there, we had to get back in the car and drive another 120 miles to Springfield, where we went to a nightclub.

It was there that I realized I was pretty far from Lorain. As I headed to the restroom, a man said to me, "The price of hogs are up."

Confused, all I could think to say was, "Pardon me?" I knew nothing about rural America.

But I was sufficiently interested to make a couple of more visits to Peoria over the next few months, although now I was traveling by air. I was enjoying my time with Lila, but didn't realize I was in love with this girl until a memorable moment at, of all places, a gas station.

She drove her father's big old Cadillac, with the outrageous fins, and stopped for gas. As I was getting a fill-up, I turned and caught a glimpse of her that I never forgot. She just glowed like an angel. For the first time, I knew I was in love with her. Whether I knew it then or not, this wasn't going to be an easy sale. This was a young woman who, two years earlier on a trip to Lebanon with her father, had been asked to enter a beauty contest on a lark, and ended up being crowned Miss Lebanon. Now, having since graduated from Bradley University and having attended a number of Orthodox conventions like the one in which I met her, she was corresponding with no fewer than three dozen other guys around the country, any one of which might beat me to her hand in marriage.

I decided to buy a ring and see if I could be first in line. I presented her with my marriage proposal by popping the question on Valentine's Day.

She promptly said, "No."

But my guardian angel was looking out for me that day, and she took the form of Lila's mother, Mae, who saw sincerity in me that her daughter didn't.

As I took the ring back and headed for the door, Mrs. Rashid stopped me with a command. She said in Arabic "Taweel bay-lak," which meant "Be patient. I'll talk to her." Then she turned to her daughter.

"Why don't you take the ring? If you don't like him, you can give it back. But he's honest."

I couldn't believe my good fortune.

Seven months later, on August 17, 1958, one year to the date of our initial meeting at that convention, Lila still had the ring and we were married. At the wedding, I had a graphic reminder of the impossibly high regard in which she was held by her extended family and circle of friends. Everyone cried, as though this were a wake and not a wedding. But in that gesture it impressed upon me even more what a gem I had found as a partner.

If the path to my eventual conversion through Billy Graham nearly 40 years later can be said to have a first step, this was certainly it. Lila was the most spiritual person I'd ever known, and the kindest. Her family was, too. After the tumultuousness of my family, I loved the difference of being around the Rashids. They were the kindest, most loving, most tender people I had ever known in my life. I was swept away by her extended family, fell in love with her cousins, her brother (a dentist, Dr. Floyd Rashid) and her dad, John Rashid, who was the kindest man I ever met. John opened grocery stores for his widowed sister and brother, Kaymel, who had fallen on hard times. Of course, I would always have a special bond with her mom, one of the wisest women I ever knew. She saw something in me worth taking a chance on when Lila was doubtful. I can never repay that debt.

They say the honeymoon is a time for newlyweds to get to really know each other. I found out right away how much faith Lila had in me. We were talking about our new life together. A lot of newlyweds start out with a nest egg, and the one we had I spent on our honeymoon in Nassau. Every penny.

Lila asked me if I knew how much money we had.

"$10."

"No, come on. You're a lawyer," she said.

"You're a teacher," I said. "How much you got?"

"Nothing."

"So we'll start together," I replied.

I had confidence. I just knew that I was going to make it, and in that I meant we were going to make it together. In those early days, I used to tease her: "You should have been a nun instead of taking care of me."

But Lila was taking care of me, in 100 ways, large and small. And by sending me Lila as a lifelong partner, the Lord was sending me perhaps His strongest signal yet: That He loved me and that He, too, was prepared to wait for me to come around.

He also sent me four wonderful children—Lisa, Fred, Janet and Lee. They would come to support me in my later years much as I supported them in their younger years.

In future years, my Lila would instill in our four children a love and appreciation for God and for the Bible. With me, she would have to take a different tack, though. She'd simply have to wait me out, providing years of good examples, patiently reminding me of what it meant to be charitable, kind and Christian. Living with Lila, I didn't need to read about or hear about what it meant to be a devout Christian. I simply had to gaze over at the person next to me in bed each night to reflect on the tremendous power of her silent example of devotion. In all the years I've known her, I can't recall a single malicious thing she's ever said.

Leo's Lesson Learned:

When you recognize the goodness in others you will soon recognize how that goodness extends to you.

CHAPTER 10

My Siblings

As I've learned to appreciate being a good Christian, the more I've reflected on the importance of family. And the more I've reflected on family, the more I've learned to better appreciate my siblings. We were all treated differently by my father. Now that may not sound unusual—it happens in a lot of families—and in those, everyone ends up receiving individualized attention. But it wasn't that way in my family.

My brother Mike was the first-born son, and my father always criticized him. He told him degrading things like, "You can't do anything right." It made Mike insecure and prone to want to please everyone. I became the ornery one who wasn't afraid of anyone or anything—except that I lived in constant fear of breaking my father's rules. My sister Joan was different. She was left to my mother as my father turned over all parenting duties to her.

Mike always pushed things under the rug. Once, I came home from college and saw the bar waitresses stuffing money in their aprons.

"Mike," I said. "What are you doing letting them do that?"

He waved me off. "Awwwww…they're just taking a few tips. Let it be, Leo."

"No, Mike. You pay them well. They don't have to do that."

"I don't care what they do," Mike said. "As long as they leave me something, it's OK."

But Mike was like that. I was the opposite. And my father never criticized me. It was always Mike being criticized. The poor guy. My father was always on his case. He wanted Mike to take the role of the Koury heir apparent, but he wouldn't. It wasn't in Mike's nature. Instead, Mike had this great, easy-going personality and wanted little to do with stressful things like taking care of the family.

I loved my brother. He was my hero. I will never forget when he came home from World War II, where he served as an aerial gunner in the Eighth Air Force over Germany. I was so happy he was safe. Two-thirds of his squadron had been killed in action, and Mike was a basket of nerves. I could see he needed some rest and relaxation.

My father, however, was rough on him. He took him over to the bar while he was still wearing his uniform.

"Dad, I want to go away to California," Mike told him. "Then I'd like to go back to Ohio University (he had a year in already)."

My father didn't answer him. He just kept going on with his business.

The next morning, when I went to see Mike, he wore a sad look on his face.

"I guess I'm not going back to college, Leo. Dad gave me $3,000 and said, 'Now you take care of the bar. I took care of five families while you were in the service. Now I'm going to California.'" And off he went.

My father loved my sister, and always treated her well. But he never showed Joan any overt affection. Of course, dad never showed affection for anyone. And when it came to Joan, he told my mother, "She's your job. Not mine."

Because of this, my father never really had a close relationship with Joan, but he didn't mistreat her. In fact, he dressed her like a princess while my mother dressed like a queen. My father was great that way—insisting on the finest clothes.

As she grew up and needed guidance, Joan ended up coming to me. I became more than her big brother, and we grew close.

Once, Joan begged me to date one of her sorority sisters. I didn't want to because I was so much older.

"Well, you know how dad is," she said, "You'd be like a chaperone for me and my friend."

So I went. That girl ended up liking me a lot. I told her I didn't have time to get involved. Again, my father just brainwashed me. I couldn't get close to girls.

Joan went on to become a teacher and met her husband, Charlie Haddad, while attending the family's church, St. George Antiochian Orthodox Church in Cleveland. Charlie was a nice gentleman and was the head of the church's governing board—he even hired and fired priests. He had a big job in personnel and was good at it. They had two children, a boy and a girl—he's a dentist and she's married to a school superintendent in Indiana.

It's funny…you never really know what you have at the time. But looking back, my siblings were great, and I loved them tremendously.

Leo's Lesson Learned:
There is nothing more important than family.

CHAPTER 11

Building a Family of Our Own

The poet Kahlil Gibran wrote in his classic work, "On Children:"

You are the bows from which your children
as living arrows are sent forth.
The archer sees the mark upon the path of the infinite,
and He bends you with His might
that His arrows may go swift and far.

I've always loved that poem. It reminds me of our family—Lila, me and our four wonderful children: Lisa, Fred, Janet and Lee. When I think about Gibran's work, I realize how relevant it is to our lives, and that Lila and I have "sent forth" our children. To our delight, they have gone swiftly to far horizons and made the two of us proud parents.

All four of our kids are high achievers—one might even say Type A personalities; at least that's what others keep telling us. And while I served as the cultivator of our family, Lila was always the bedrock, the foundation our children needed to remain grounded.

Lisa, our oldest, was born in 1959, a year after Lila and I were married. She, along with two of our other children, Fred and Janet, graduated from the former Admiral King High School in Lorain, a public school. After graduation, Lisa headed off to Bowling Green State University to make her mark on the world. But she was unhappy there—as well as homesick—and transferred to Baldwin-Wallace College so she could commute from home, and earned her business degree.

Lisa met her future husband, Jim Faro, at the 1980 Democratic National Convention in New York City. I had known Jim's parents through a business association and invited them to join our family at the convention. Who could have predicted the two would hit it off and eventually marry?

In 1982, after Lisa and Jim married, she attended interior decorating school and launched a career in the industry. Jim went into the seafood industry, where he's been a very successful entrepreneur. The two of them moved to Boston and raised their three children on the East Coast.

Lisa and Jim gave Lila and me three grandchildren. Their oldest, Richard, lives in San Francisco and works in the high-tech industry. He married a lovely woman named Corey. Next came Jennifer. She fell in love with and married a former U.S. Coast Guard officer and current financial adviser with Edward Jones, Brian Yurovich, who hailed from Lorain. Lisa and Jim's youngest child Stephanie graduated from George Washington University and works for a leasing company in New York City. Each of them is doing well and we couldn't be more proud.

Our eldest son, Fred, was born in 1963. He was a nice kid, and everybody liked him. During the summers, I would make all of our children get jobs so that they would learn about the importance of responsibility. Fred would always delegate his job. He was already a smart, budding entrepreneur back then—he was the shrewdest of all my kids—and that entrepreneurial spirit would blossom the older he got.

After college, Fred went to work with Jim, his brother-in-law, in the fish business and became a star salesman. He didn't really like the life of a salesman on the road—even though he was doing well—and sought out a change.

I gave Fred a Nissan 300 red sports car as a graduation present. In 1989, he sold it to fund a business he and two partners founded—Smart Business Network. The three of them started publishing a 16-page magazine every other month that served Cleveland-area small businesses. Over the next few years, Fred's business grew. He bought out his partners and transformed the company. Today, the company has grown and branched out into other services. He's really become a great entrepreneur.

Fred married a beautiful woman, Lena, whom he met through his company. They've given Lila and me two amazing grandsons, Joseph and Michael. I see Fred nearly every day as my office is right next to his in Smart Business' building. How great is that?

Our third child, Janet, was born in 1964. She also went to Baldwin-Wallace College and studied communications and business. In 1990 she joined her brother Fred at Smart Business Network. Today, she is the company's vice president for business development, and I see her all the time as well.

In 2007, Janet married Anthony Valore, president of Valore Builders Inc., a regional homebuilder and developer. The two of them are wonderful. She teaches Bible studies both in home and at church; she also has written more than 900 Christian songs, poems and children's books.

Our youngest, Lee, was born in 1972. He was the only one of our four children to attend a private high school. Lee was an excellent student and enjoyed his studies. We embraced this and enrolled him at Lorain Catholic High School to give him a top-notch education. Not surprisingly, Lee graduated second in his class.

Beyond his academics, Lee also excelled in sports. He earned 10 letters during his high school days and then went on to earn a bachelor's degree in business administration, with distinction, in finance and marketing from the University of Michigan's School of Business Administration. Then, Lee followed in my footsteps and became a lawyer, earning his law degree from Case Western Reserve University School of Law. Lee and his beautiful wife, Gretchen, have four children: Eli, Halle, Annie and Lila. They are all such a joy to have around.

Lee spent several years working as a lawyer at a well-known firm in Cleveland before leaving and joining Fred at Smart Business Network, where he's become one of the managing partners. He, too, is a daily part of my life.

Looking back on our time with our children, the secret to raising them the way we did started with Lila. While I was hardly ever home because I was always looking for the next deal, Lila taught them manners, responsibility in the house and how to treat people. Because of Lila's dedication to our children, each one was able to become self-reliant and eventually pursue their individual passions. And, while I was the disciplinarian, Lila was the compassionate one—she taught them the most important lesson of all: how to love. She never raised her voice…yet, they always listened.

Lila also attended to our children's religious training. Growing up, she went to a Catholic school and frequently attended church. That's why I'm still amazed to this day that we ever met. Lila and I were complete opposites. Our lives—specifically when it came to religion—should not have intersected. It wasn't until the day we attended the Billy Graham Crusade that my life transformed and became better aligned with how Lila saw the world and was teaching our children to view it.

While I was a sinner, Lila was always tolerant of my mischievousness and lack of Christianity. She was always trying to get me to embrace the Lord. It wasn't until 1994 that this would happen. And unbeknownst to me, our children would become key players in this transformation. Fred was at the same Billy Graham Crusade. Janet was there with a friend. None of us knew the others were going.

If there's one thing I've learned so far in my life, it's that family is so important. I'm blessed to have such an amazing, close-knit family. But such is the way with God's intervention. He, like Lila, was there for our children—always. And, when it counted most, He was always there for me, too.

Leo's Lesson Learned:
You can be the cultivator for family, but your wife will be the bedrock.

CHAPTER 12

Friendship and Partings

As much as my father cared about the downtrodden—which were often poor immigrants—so did I. And so I got involved in several activities around town. My father taught me well, but little did I know that this caring nature was really God's way of letting me know what was really important in life. The Bible says, "What does it profit a man if he gains the world and loses his soul." I wasn't thinking about this at the time, but looking back, it was just another example of Him influencing my decisions.

As a result, I engaged in numerous community-oriented activities that benefited more than just our growing family. One of those initiatives was joining a committee that created the Lorain International Festival in 1966. The goal of the festival was to celebrate the diverse cultural heritage of the "International City." There were events, entertainment, ethnic foods, crafts and a parade. We even selected a festival queen. It was a grand program, and the community loved it—55 different ethnicities participated. I was honored to serve as the festival's second president.

Around the same time, I also was asked to become a director with ALSAC, Aiding Leukemia-Stricken American Children, also known as American Lebanese Syrian Associated Charities. Through contacts I was able to bring Danny Thomas, the founder of St. Jude Children's Research Hospital, to Lorain. We raised a substantial amount of money for the organization before the hospital in Memphis was built and Danny became a good friend. ALSAC is one of the greatest charities I've ever been involved with, and I continue to support it today.

If there's one thing you need to keep in mind about your heritage it's that you should build on your ancestry. Everything leads back to it.

As my involvement with community-based nonprofit organizations grew, so did the joy I received from giving back. And though

I didn't realize it at the time, the more I gave back the more people took notice. Eventually, I got involved with politics—serving as a delegate to the Democratic National Convention in 1976 and 1980. I was also able to later tap into an army of volunteers that would later become crucial regional support for Jimmy Carter's election.

The greatest benefit of everything I became involved with, however, wasn't the recognition. It was the friends I made along the way. This includes my best friend, Pasquale "Patsie" Campana Sr., who was a lifelong friend.

Patsie and I first met on the playground of Harrison Elementary School. I was being bullied and he came to my rescue. Patsie told the bully to leave me alone, and the bully backed down. Ever since then, Patsie was my hero.

We lost touch over the years, as friends often do, but in the late 1960s we reconnected. Mill Tavern was destroyed by a fire that started next door, and I needed advice on building an office building on the spot—to keep my father's legacy alive. Patsie, who had a construction company, helped me develop the Koury Building, which in 1970 was dedicated in my dad's memory.

As my legal career grew, I started to better understand my strengths and weaknesses. Maybe I wasn't the greatest lawyer in the world, but I had earned credibility from others for doing the right thing. Respect goes a long way in this world, and when you combine that with humility it can become pretty powerful. My father taught me that—even if I hadn't realized it at the time. It was yet another example of God watching over me.

Patsie and I remained close friends from then on—our families became close as well. I can't say the same for Joe Ujhelyi. Joe and I started growing apart in 1978 when I helped launch the Dr. Alfred J. Loser Memorial Scholarship.

The Dr. Alfred J. Loser Memorial Scholarship is still in existence today, and has grown from its initial seed money of $260,000 to more than $1.7 million. More than 2,000 kids have benefited from the foundation by going to college. These are students who not only had high grades but were from humble households below the poverty line. The only requirement for the scholarships was that the students had to return to Lorain to give back to the community. We wanted people to pay it forward—another of the Lord's great lessons.

Dr. Loser was an amazing man. He originally had an office on Pearl Avenue in Lorain, not far from Mill Tavern, and used to give me shots and never charge me for them. Dr. Loser made a large bequest to the Lorain schools so students could receive college scholarships—this is what eventually turned into the foundation.

He was a bachelor. Lila and I would invite him over for dinner, and he took a liking to us. Dr. Loser was a real gentleman. He studied in Vienna, Austria, and was a brilliant diagnostician. He primarily took care of the Hungarian community, but wasn't received well outside that population because he was a foreigner and had an accent.

One day, he called me because his office space—and my office as well; we were in the same building—was changing hands and he had to move. At the time he was 75, and didn't want to retire. In fact, he was still making house calls.

Joe wanted us all to go to the Slovenian National Home, where there was office space, and make it a "Little Hungary" or "Little Budapest." That would be a suitable place for the doctor's new office. But that wasn't in the cards.

At this point of the story, "The Prophet," by endeared Lebanese poet Khalil Gibran, comes to mind as a way to explain what happened next.

In the story, the prophet is about to sail back to his homeland after 12 years in a city—they were not happy years. He was a stranger—an outsider—who never was accepted. But a surprising thing happens: People pour from their homes to join him in his walk to the harbor. In his years there, he had won the respect and love of the people, yet he never knew it until then.

With that as inspiration I began thinking differently about solutions. Because Mill Tavern had burned down, I envisioned on that spot an office building for myself and others, including Dr. Loser—the outsider who was a humanitarian and philanthropist. My friend, Patsie, helped make this idea a reality.

When Dr. Loser fell ill a few years later, he called me from the hospital and wanted me to write his will. I told him I couldn't, but that it would be appropriate for our friend Joe to do the legal work, not me. But Dr. Loser didn't see it that way. As a result, the two of them eventually got into an argument that ended when they started hollering at each other in Hungarian.

I finally said, "I don't want any part of this. I don't want to come between you two."

But Dr. Loser insisted that I write his will because of all the good things I had done for him. Despite my protests, I acquiesced, and that decision upset Joe.

"Go ahead take care of it," he finally told me, trying to hide his emotions. But I could see he was clearly hurt by the decision. This was a man from his era that built up his world, and now I was the new generation and didn't realize it.

Shortly thereafter, I moved Dr. Loser's equipment to the Koury Building and set up his office nice and neat. I had his name on the door and everything. He was so shocked and pleased when he saw it that he started crying like a baby because he thought it was all over for him when he lost his old office.

As a thank you, Dr. Loser bought a bottle of the finest champagne and presented it to me. I didn't drink champagne, but from that time on he kept calling me to stay in touch.

I had great admiration for Dr. Loser, but there were other heroes in my life besides the people who were physically close to me, including statesman Gen. George Marshall. Both Marshall and my father followed the credo: "Constant honesty creates instant credibility."

I became obsessed with Marshall and read everything I could find on him. At one point, Patsie's son, Bob, chartered a jet and with several friends and I flew to Lexington, Virginia, to visit the Marshall Museum. I guess I talked so much about Marshall on the way down to the museum that I wore the group out—that's how much influence the man had on my life.

It was exciting to visit the museum and see all the information and artifacts about his remarkable life. We even saw the Nobel Peace Prize Marshall received in 1953 for his contributions toward restoring the European economy through the Marshall Plan. It was truly an amazing day.

Winston Churchill is another of my heroes. He saved England and always had a great command of the English language. Among my favorite Churchill sayings is "We shall fight on the beaches, we shall fight on the landing grounds, we shall fight in the fields and in the streets, we shall fight in the hills; we shall never surrender. I have nothing to offer but blood, toil, tears and sweat."

I remember reading about his life and the time a woman said to him, "If you were my husband, I'd poison your coffee." Churchill famously quipped back, "If you were my wife, I'd drink it, and I may be drunk, Miss, but in the morning I will be sober and you will still be ugly." It was a great example of his humor.

With people like Patsie, George Marshall, Winston Churchill, and my father as heroes in my life, I began to think about how to become more like them. It got me thinking more about the power of giving back and doing the right thing—the more you give, the more good things come your way.

When Patsie passed away in 1993, it felt like a part of me died with him. At his funeral at St. Peter's Church in Lorain, I gave tribute to my friend through a eulogy. Looking back, I still think about Patsie. Not long ago I ran across the eulogy I had written. And as I read the words I spoke about my friend more than two decades earlier, I realized those words—and the man—meant as much to me today as they did then:

This will probably be the toughest speech I ever gave. That's something for a lawyer to say, but it is a eulogy of my best friend.

I am fortunate that I am able to say that I had a best friend. Not many people can say that in their lifetime. The dictionary defines a friend as a person who likes another, a companion, a comrade, a chum. My definition of PC was to know all of his faults and still love him, and he the same of me.
I had the privilege of knowing him since my childhood. However, our paths went in different directions for several years, he into the Navy and throughout the world in steel mills. What people don't know about was his courage in the Navy as a deep-sea diver. He would never tell you, but I found out from family

and friends, how he landed at Iwo Jima and volunteered to retrieve under fire the bodies of our servicemen and bring them back so they could be buried. As you know, Iwo Jima was one of our biggest losses in our campaign during World War II. He also dove at Tokyo Bay to clear up landmines and other things.

PC was truly one of a kind. A very unique human being. In fact, he had more humanity and love for his family and friends and strangers in need than any man I knew. As you all know, he was born in Abruzzo, Italy, in the Apennine Mountains, and came to America as an infant. He was often proud of his heritage and he used to say to me, a man who denies his heritage has none; he is without culture or family.

He gave the appearance of a common ordinary working man. He had an explosive temper when he felt a person was not true or fair to anyone. But his intemperance was short-lived and forgiving. His greatest quality was that he had character, his honesty his industry, his loyalty and his courage. Patsie was a very humble and generous man. He was the true philanthropist, always helping churches, schools, hospitals, organizations and many needy people. Right now, he would be embarrassed and would want to clip me for even talking about it.

He personified the American dream, as Dick Callella [a previous speaker] said; a first generation American of immigrant parents who was self-educated by hard work and on-the-job training, always relating to when he was a welder at the American shipyard, then an electrician, then a foreman and then a superintendent, never faltering or goofing off but always learning. A man with that background to become a giant in the steel industry is the most remarkable achievement that this community will ever see.

The remarkable thing about him was that at the age of 48, leaving the security as the head of the company, having six children, he started on his own from scratch to build this empire that you see today. Truly the captain of industry.

He was the most caring and concerned person about his brother Baldo, Albert, Rosemary, and their families' needs, always talking to me about them, grateful to Rosemary for taking care of mom, so he could get the things accomplished to take care of the rest of the family. He loved his wife Jenee, his daughter Patti Ann, sons David, Larry, Bobby, Scotty, Corky and all his grandchildren, more than life itself. He was a big pussycat. He didn't want anybody to know it.

I offer a challenge today to all the family and friends in the words of President John F. Kennedy on this 30th anniversary of his death from his inaugural address that should apply to all of you. We dare not forget today that you are the heirs of PC Campana. Let the word go forth from this time and place to friends and foe alike that the torch has been passed to a new generation of Campanas, born in this century, tempered by hard work, disciplined by a taskmaster father, proud of his Italian heritage and unwilling to witness or permit the deterioration of all his hard work and success. Let every person know whether a fellow worker or a competitor, whether they wish you well or ill, that you are the heirs, will pay any price, bear any burden, meet any hardship, support any friends, oppose any foe to ensure the survival of the P.C. Campana Group and its continued success. One for all and all for one is the pledge to the memory of your father.

And to you, friends, Saturdays will never be the same at Tiffany's Restaurant for Frank Provenza, Karel Fiser, Tony LaRizza, Dr. Janay Fiserova and myself. However, I would also like to acknowledge one of his dearest friends who honors the Campana family to appear here, Attorney General Lee Fisher, who is one of the few public officials that Patsie could stand. Patsie would point a finger at him and lecture him and talk to him like he was talking to a member of the family. And the brilliant Lee Fisher would sit there and listen. Whether he was listening or not we never knew but at least he gave him the appearance. Thank you, Lee.

And to the friends, I offer a passage from the Rubaiyat of Omar Khayyam, as you know, is from my side of the Mediterranean.

'The Moving Finger writes; and, having writ,
Moves on: nor all thy Piety nor Wit
Shall lure it back to cancel half a Line,
Nor all thy Tears wash out a Word of it.'

And the last thing I could say is what was said to me when my father died after a brief career and life and died at the age of 47, I buried him on my 23rd birthday, there is nothing else we can say at this time except to go forth, family and friends, and be the person he would have wanted you to be so that they look at you and say, 'There is Patsie's children, there is Patsie's friend and his name carries on.' He will live in my heart till the day I die. God rest his soul.

The lesson is that friendship isn't something to be taken lightly. It's one of the greatest lessons I learned in my life. Patsie taught me that.

Leo's Lesson Learned:
Speechless was my love, and with veils has it been veiled.
Yet now it cries aloud to you. Love knows not its own depth until the hour of separation.

CHAPTER 13
Kingmaking

I began my dizzying journey from life's virtual outhouse to the nation's White House by reading a brief magazine item about an obscure, blue-eyed peanut farmer and former Georgia governor named James Earl Carter.

Previously, I left the politics to Joe Ujhelyi. He was, after all, the county Democratic chairman. But my success helping to launch the Lorain International Festival gave me a workable business model for using grass-roots support to pay off at the ballot box. After all, my father did more than rub elbows with politicians; why shouldn't I?

It was in late December 1974, deep into the pre-holiday season, and I happened to be trolling through *Time* magazine when I stopped to read about the politician who insisted on being called "Jimmy" Carter.

Jimmy Carter had just become the second Democrat to announce his candidacy for president of the United States.

"Although he has cultivated a reformer's image by declining campaign contributions larger than $1,000 and has dutifully stumped for fellow Democrats in 32 states this year as [Democratic National Committee Congressional] chairman, Carter will have hard work to make his name recognized by more voters and to build support for himself in Democratic organizations outside Georgia," the article noted.

As I read the account, it hit me what his political strategy was: Carter was doing all this traveling and fundraising for other candidates in order to gather favors for his own campaign. Shades of something my father would have done. In the sour national political climate of the moment, poisoned as it was by Richard Nixon and the Watergate scandal, I knew that despite his low-name recognition, Carter had a couple of important things going for him, besides his evidently strong work ethic.

For one thing, he was a Washington outsider, and for another, he was religious and didn't hide his Christian beliefs. Even though

I hadn't come to Christ yet, the latter fact was something that still didn't escape me.

One evening, we were hosting a holiday party at our home. As I made the rounds passing out drinks and appetizers to my guests, I came upon Joe and a couple of local judges talking about their favorite candidates in the presidential race. Joe was squarely behind the party's favorite candidate, Hubert Humphrey, while one of the judges was in the corner of a challenger, Indiana's Birch Bayh. Another guest that night voiced his support for Arizona's popular political maverick, "Mo" Udall.

I, however, piped up in support of my man.

"No, your next president is going to be Jimmy Carter."

"Who?" they asked. Almost two years away from the election, Carter's name wasn't well-known, even among such political insiders as these.

Someone must have mentioned my comments. Not long afterward, I got a call from a local operative of the Carter campaign, a Clevelander named Christine Gitlin. She had learned of my pro-Carter comments, and asked if I'd like to work for his campaign.

"Now why would I want to do that?" I asked her, petulant as always to someone I didn't know. After all, except for my campaign efforts in support of the J. William "Bill" McCray congressional race a decade and a half earlier, I had been strictly working on local campaigns. In an attempt to get rid of her, I left the door partly open for her invitation. "Tell him if he comes to Lorain, Ohio, I will consider it."

Instead, she countered with the possibility of a meeting with the candidate in his hometown of Plains, Georgia.

Fine, I thought. I'll set up a test that he'll be destined to fail. I'll bring some of my union-leader clients along and see how this southern governor of a pro-management right-to-work state addresses their concerns about labor issues.

"If he can convince them, maybe I'll do it," I told her.

Suddenly, I found myself on a southbound flight in a small turbo-prop aircraft owned by one of my clients. Since tiny Plains, home to just 600 people, didn't even have an airport, we landed on a grass field, bouncing all along.

As we made our way from the makeshift landing field to Carter's home, I couldn't believe what I was seeing. The town looked like something out of a movie about the Wild West. There was a single street bisecting an almost empty little hamlet. We saw a corrugated metal shack with a sign out front: It was a gas station that belonged to Jimmy's brother, Billy. And then we came upon the most incredible sight yet: A prison chain gang working on the side of the road. The prisoners actually wore striped uniforms. The men were chained to each other and shackled. I thought this kind of treatment of prisoners had gone out in the Dark Ages.

When we finally got to Carter's farm, I was in for a surprise. I let my union friends, John Hunter, president of United Auto Workers Locals 425 and 2000, and Lonnie Mullins, treasurer, do most of the talking, and they all but cross-examined Carter on labor issues. (Today, John is the mayor of Sheffield Village, a small west side suburb of Cleveland.)

Carter was unruffled.

He wasn't against unions, but he thought right-to-work should mean everyone should have the right to choose a union or not. Darned if he didn't convince them. One by one, he won over these hardened union men. In fact, they went wild for him.

As we left, I was struck by Carter's simple appearance. He didn't look like a presidential candidate so much as he did a simple farmer. Like my dad's practice of putting an expensive suit on a deserving person, I almost felt the urge to buy him a suit out of pity for the cheap-looking polyester one he was wearing. At the same time, I was struck by his deep humility. Having read about his military background as an engineer on a nuclear submarine program under famed U.S. Navy Adm. Hyman Rickover, I knew he had to be smart and shrewd. At a subconscious level, although I hadn't yet committed my life to Christ, I must've been deeply struck by his profoundly Christian decency. I think it helped me gravitate toward him.

Regardless, I didn't think our visit would amount to much. As we prepared to leave Plains that day, not only did I decline again to contribute to the campaign, but I made it clear to Carter's people that I wouldn't work for the campaign unless Carter arranged a visit to Lorain. I really never thought he would.

This would be my first of several miscalculations about Jimmy Carter.

A few weeks later, back in Lorain, I received another call from my liaison to the Carter campaign, Christine Gitlin.

"Leo, when would you like Carter in Lorain?"

"You're kidding," I said.

"No. Can you set up a fundraiser?"

"Let me talk to my people, and I'll get back to you," I told her.

I quickly called Bill McCray, some leaders of the steelworkers union and a few other key people who had worked on earlier campaigns with me. They were enthusiastic about Carter's candidacy. Suddenly, I had the makings of the only countywide organization for a presidential candidate. That's because as a rule, Joe Ujhelyi studiously avoided getting involved in primaries. This year would be no different. To avoid the pleading of various candidates, Joe would instead take his ritual six-week trip to Tucson, Arizona, where he took in the Cleveland Indians' spring training games. Then, he'd return to the political battle he loved so well, to put all his resources behind whatever Democrats had emerged victorious from the primaries. So here was a political vacuum that I was left to fill.

Everything I had learned in years of organizing political campaigns would be brought to bear with my support for Jimmy Carter. All of my wide friendships—unions and various nationalities across Lorain—would help, as would the fact that people naturally tended to gather around me. I began getting people together to support Carter.

Over the years I had become good friends with Father Bruce Ward, an Irish-American Catholic priest who was pastor of Sacred Heart, the largest Hispanic parish in the city. He agreed to let the church serve as the site for the main program, an action for which he later caught an earful from his superiors. I lined up the local Holiday Inn to host a unique series of fundraising receptions. We were off and running.

In late May 1976, just a week before the all-important Ohio presidential primary, Carter finally paid his visit to Lorain.

We packed close to 2,000 people into the church for Carter's speech. He thrilled the crowd when he spoke a little Spanish. The appearance even made the national TV news. But the hotel fundraisers that were held before the church address were the key to the visit.

It was there, at the private fundraisers, that I was able to blend my style of people power for the masses with the need to raise the maximum amount of dollars possible. We had settled on a three-pronged approach: In the suites, we hosted a private cocktail reception for $1,000 contributors. Then, we went down a floor to a meeting room, where a wider group of union leaders and others of more middling means paid $100 for the privilege of rubbing elbows with the candidate. Finally, in the ballroom, grass-roots campaign workers and others of more modest resources gathered for a party at $10 a head. It was this group which especially went crazy for Carter, because it's not every day that a viable presidential candidate reaches out to so many average voters. Even though Carter wasn't really the warm and charismatic type, everyone could sense that he was down-to-earth.

"How much money did you raise for him?" an attractive young national TV reporter named Judy Woodruff asked me.

"I don't handle that," I responded.

Richard Threlkeld from CBS's national desk was there, too. He was covering the story of the up-and-coming long shot candidate who was wooing crowds in Lorain, Ohio.

Actually, I had fibbed to Woodruff. When the receipts were told from the day, we had raised more than $30,000 for Jimmy Carter. That might not sound like much today, when top-tier presidential candidates must raise tens of millions of dollars just to be competitive. But in the early post-Watergate era, when the 1974 Federal Elections Campaign Act opened a new vista for lesser-known candidates and before so-called "soft-money" loopholes opened the way to millions in corporate contributions, this was a lot of money.

The new campaign finance law, passed in the wake of popular revulsion over President Nixon's satchels of campaign cash, capped individual contributions to presidential candidates at $1,000 apiece. For the first time, it allowed long-shot candidates such as Carter—who readily admitted he would never have been able to run but for the new law—to compete by emphasizing grass-roots giving over large contributions from a few wealthy individuals.

In order to qualify for federal matching funds under this law, a candidate had to raise just $5,000 in each of 20 states with gifts of $250 or less. Carter once ordered his son Chip to go to Texas for fundraising and not to return until he had $5,000. In this context, $30,000 grabbed a lot of people's attention.

Still, corralling votes was more important. As late as the spring of 1976, the former Georgia governor was still in a tight race for the party nomination. Though Carter had handily won his first two primary season contests, the Iowa caucuses and the New Hampshire primary, that success planted the seeds for a strong "Stop Carter" movement in the party.

The final round of primaries was scheduled for June 8, with the large states of California, Ohio and New Jersey all due to go to polls. With the Democratic nominee still in doubt, this was shaping up as the most important day of the former peanut farmer's long race for the White House.

Ohio really shined that day. In fact, Ohio helped transform the Carter campaign into the Carter presidency. As First Lady Rosalynn Carter would later recount in her memoir, "First Lady from Plains," it was Ohio that sealed the nomination for Jimmy Carter:

> That night when the returns came in, we had lost in New Jersey and lost in California, but we won in Ohio! Ohio had come through for us, and Ohio was what we needed. I was numb, and I think I cried from sheer exhaustion and relief. It was over. This part of it was over. We have broken our losing streak with the one victory we had to have. When Ohio came in, Jimmy kissed me and said, 'We did it, and we'll win the nomination now on the first ballot!'

That summer, at the Democratic National Convention in New York's Madison Square Garden, Ohio was once more a symbolic key to formal victory. As Rosalynn later recalled, the suspense was building late that night:

Which state would put us over the top? It was Massachusetts'
turn [to report their delegates]. 'Massachusetts passes.' Next was
Ohio. 'Ohio casts 132 votes for Carter!' Ohio had done it again.

Finally, there was the last hurdle: Election night.

I was in Atlanta, Georgia, waiting for the returns along with hundreds of other key campaign workers. When the television networks flashed the news that Ohio was building toward a 10,000-vote victory for Carter (all of it, we later learned, accounted for by an even wider plurality of 13,000 votes in Lorain County), everyone cheered.

If one state could be said to have won Jimmy Carter the presidency, it was probably Ohio. And if one of Ohio's 88 counties was the key to that victory, it was no doubt Lorain. And who had worked so feverishly to deliver the vote there? My head was beginning to swell a little, as I began to silently speculate about a juicy White House appointment someday soon as thanks for my efforts in the field. Again, my lack of humility in those days goes without saying.

And so, I went home to Lorain early that November convinced that the life of this son of a bootlegger was about to become considerably more interesting still.

Leo's Lesson Learned:
The toughest times don't last forever; but the toughest people do.

CHAPTER 14

Life Becomes a Blur

The next four years, coinciding with the Carter presidency, would soon become a blur. There were tantalizing suggestions of high government appointments and chances to meet some of the most interesting and famous people in the world. In the process, I would be grilled by the Senate Foreign Relations Committee and submit to an exhaustive FBI background check. But there were plenty of perks. I attended international trade conferences, was invited to meet the Pope, and best of all helped with the historic 1978 ceremony at Camp David that marked the Arab-Israeli peace treaty.

It all began memorably with our visit to Washington for the Inaugural festivities. It was so cold that January day that our guests, my best friend Patsie Campana and his wife Jenee, decided to stay indoors for the Inaugural parade. But the forbidding weather didn't prevent the new First Family from following through on their famous popular statement: a stroll down Pennsylvania Avenue.

We stayed in a hotel just one floor below the president's infamous brother Billy, who convened the most raucous—if least formal—of all the Inaugural gatherings. Everyone was swigging beer, barefoot.

One day, while kibitzing with Vice President Walter Mondale's aide Dick Moe, Moe brought up a possible appointment as ambassador to the United Arab Emirates. A diplomat! I sure liked the ring of that. My head began to swell a bit, but my family quickly dashed the idea. When I told them the news, they immediately cried. They weren't interested in moving overseas. More importantly, they were worried about my safety.

Over the next several months, the newspapers speculated about various plums I would be offered.

"In Washington, Columbus and Cleveland, some of the Jimmy Carter guys are saying that Cleveland Councilman George Forbes and Lorain attorney Leo Koury are among the choices for the federal district attorney in Cleveland," one columnist wrote.

That one never came to pass, but I did decline one formal offer—a position in Cincinnati overseeing the savings and loan industry.

While I was biding my time, we received an invitation from the secretary to First Lady Rosalynn Carter to a White House dinner. I didn't want to go, but Lila was interested.

"You never cared about politics," I said.

"But I want to see Egyptian President Anwar Sadat's wife, Jehan," Lila said. "They tell me she's beautiful, and it's an honor. They tell me there's only so many people all over the world being invited, and I'd love to go."

She was right—as usual. It was an honor to be invited, so we decided to accept and attend the dinner.

One week earlier, the same secretary called me to serve as an intermediary between the Democratic women and the Republican women in Lorain because the First Lady was coming to certify the Palace Theatre as a national landmark.

"Why do you want me?" I asked.

"Because there's friction between the two. The Republican women are in charge and the Democratic women are upset. We want you to straighten it out."

Once more, I agreed to help. This was a week before the White House dinner. I set up the Democratic women to meet with the First Lady at the Holiday Inn before going to the Palace Theatre; and then afterward a meeting with the Republican women.

After it was done, First Lady Rosalynn Carter's advance man thanked me for solving a sensitive problem and put something in my pocket.

Later, I pulled it out to see what he had placed in my pocket—it was a presidential pin.

When we finally went to the dinner in Washington, I put on the pin. It turned out that it opened doors wherever I went. Because I wore that coveted pin we were at the table next to the president and the dignitaries from Israel and Egypt that were involved in the famous Middle East peace talks. Carter famously brokered those talks, which led to the peace deal. For security reasons, however, no one was permitted to go up and talk to them at the dinner.

My wife, being a bit naive, got up and proceed to approach the table next to us. She wanted to meet Jehan.

I stood up immediately to grab her so she wouldn't get embarrassed. When the security people saw my pin, especially the Secret Service, they said, "He's OK."

To my surprise, they let the two of us through. I walked up to Sadat and said to him in Arabic, "Ahlan wa sahlan," which loosely translated means "Welcome."

He broke out in a big smile because he saw few Middle Easterners at the event. Most of the attendees were Jewish or gentile. I kissed Sadat on each cheek, as is the custom, and he kissed me back. We exchanged greetings with his wife, Jehan. The two of them were thrilled to have someone speak to them in their native language.

After greeting the Egyptian president, Lila and I approached President Carter. I congratulated him on the Camp David Summit and he gave me a weak handshake. But then I said, "It was an honor having your wife in Lorain the week before." And at that, the president clutched me harder—he loved his wife so much and wanted to show his appreciation for my help with her visit.

After shaking hands with the president, I decided to speak with Menachem Begin, then-prime minister of Israel. Honestly, I had nothing but hostility toward this man because of his extreme views. I had read that even Jewish leadership didn't like him. But we introduced ourselves anyway.

"My wife is a former Miss Lebanon," I said as I shook his hand.

"Miss Lebanon?" he said. "She should be Miss Universe!"

Lila kicked me.

Then I said, "You know, you and I are brothers."

At this time in my life I wasn't yet reading the Bible, but I knew a little. "Yes," I said. "We have the same father."

"Who's that?" the prime minister asked.

"Abraham," I replied.

The prime minister smiled. "You're a smart man, my son," he said. Then he kissed me on both cheeks and gave me a hug.

After that, Ezer Weizman, Israeli minister of defense, came up and started talking to me in Arabic. I was shocked.

"How do you know Arabic?" I asked.

"My father used to take me to Beirut," he said. "I heard you were

Lebanese. I'd like to invite you to visit us in Israel."

"When there's peace in Lebanon, I'd be happy to come to Israel," I replied.

Weizman was an impressive man. He was well-rounded, and objective.

"Are you coming to Camp David?" he asked.

"No," I said. "They didn't invite me to that one. I'm too outspoken."

"That's a shame," he said. "You'd be great."

"Well, I heard you're great, too," I said. "Because you're so objective."

"Thank you," he said, and then he left.

It was a great honor to meet the prime minister and others that night. Looking back, it's still hard to believe that a small-town lawyer from Lorain was invited to be part of such a group of people.

A few years later, while attending an international trade conference at the Waldorf Astoria New York, I met a Carter insider, the wealthy businessman J. Bruce Llewellyn. Bruce took a liking to me and I was invited to lunch with him at Manhattan's fabled Rainbow Room.

Over lunch, Bruce told me that the best place to blend my ethnic heritage and my interest in overseas business would be a seat on the board of OPIC (Overseas Private Investment Corp.). While little-known and underpaying, $1 a year in fact, the quasi-governmental body serves a crucial function, providing risk insurance for U.S. companies doing business internationally and otherwise encouraging exports. For me, a seat on the board would mean a chance to meet and rub elbows with some uniquely powerful and interesting people while continuing to practice law in Lorain. With Bruce pushing for me, I was formally nominated by the White House to replace Wallace Bennett, whose term was expiring. My term, if I was confirmed, would run until 1983. Ironically, this was the same seat once held years earlier by Nixon moneyman Maurice Stans, who had gone to prison for his role in Watergate.

All through the fall I watched with growing concern as Carter's re-election campaign was in full battle mode. It was late in the process, and I knew that if Carter lost to his Republican challenger, Ronald Reagan, my nomination would probably be scotched. It had been months since the announcement and I still hadn't appeared before the Senate Foreign Relations Committee for a formal hearing on my appointment.

As the election neared, the entire Ohio delegation—about 200 of us—was invited to the White House. Hamilton Jordan, White House chief of staff, said, "Well, we've got to raise money now for the President's birthday." He meant re-election.

On my left was Frank Celeste, Ohio Governor Richard Celeste's father; on my right was Ohio Attorney General Anthony Celebrezze. I raised my hand. As soon as I raised my hand, both of them moved away from me a little bit. They knew I was outspoken.

"Yes, what's your pleasure?" Jordan said.

"Do you know my name?" I said.

"Well, you're from Ohio," he said.

"Brilliant, we're all from Ohio. You know, I like the president. I'm going to vote for the president. I'll give him a contribution. But I can't raise him any money because you all forgot who brought you here."

And then I stood up and walked out.

Later, everybody told me, "Leo, you blew it after all these years." But I had been waiting four years for the White House to acknowledge the hard work we did in getting the president elected. I was done waiting, so I walked out.

As I reached the door, an aide stopped me and said, "Somebody wants to talk to you on the phone."

It was Bob Strauss, chairman of the committee to re-elect Carter. This was important because that relationship was really great.

I picked up the phone. "Leo, this is Bob Strauss. We need to talk."

"Yes, Mr. Strauss."

"Call me Bob."

"No, I have too much respect for you. I'll stick with Mr. Strauss."

"OK. Leo, I'm next door at the executive office building. I would like to speak to you. I don't want you to go away without me having a chance to talk to you."

"For you, Mr. Strauss, I'll come over."

In Strauss' office we sat down and began to talk. He asked me what the problem was, and why I was so down on the president and the re-election campaign.

"Look, I like the president. But his people, they're fighting the Civil War all over again because they're from the South. When we come to meetings at your building here, they wear high-top shoes and jeans, not respecting the protocol—they're letting Washington know that they're running the show."

"OK," he said.

"Mr. Strauss, I like the president," I reiterated. "But his people, they're killing him. And he's got the wrong people around him... except you. That's why I'm here."

"Leo," he said. "I appreciate your candor. But what's your real problem?"

"Well, my appointment for OPIC was announced a year ago and nothing's formally happened since."

He said, "You mean you haven't been before the Senate of Foreign Relations Committee?"

"No," I said, and within seconds he had then-Sen. Joe Biden on the phone. That's the kind of power he had.

"Joe, I've got Leo Koury here. He's going to go back to Cleveland unless we get him before your committee tomorrow."

"No problem," Biden said.

The next day, at the hearing, there was a problem. Massachusetts Democrat Paul Tsongas opened the hearing by taking issue with the political nature of my appointment.

I responded that my background putting together a nationality fair with 55 ethnic groups had prepared me for the post. Tsongas even blasted me for being a lawyer, of which there were too many.

"Sen. Tsongas," I said, once I had the opportunity to respond. "I got married in the Greek Orthodox Church. I'm godfather to Greek children, and I'm a member of the national American Hellenic Educational Progressive Association. Is that good enough for you?"

Everybody was smirking. The senator turned red and shut up. Committee chairman Sen. Biden winked at me.

Then it was North Carolina's irascible conservative, Sen. Jesse Helms' turn. He was a folksier interrogator, but he nevertheless made it clear that my nomination wasn't going anywhere. He was sure that my patron, Carter, was about to lose his quest for another term, and had no trouble saying so. But this merely provided former astronaut John Glenn, then a U.S. senator from Ohio, an opening to come to my defense in ringing fashion.

In a gesture I'll never forget, Glenn came down from the dais where he had been sitting with other committee members, and sat next to me.

"Leo Koury is one of the finest people I know," he said.

Despite Helms' concerns, the committee unanimously voted to approve me and to send my nomination to the full Senate.

Glenn, meanwhile, continued to push for me behind the scenes. In late August, I got a note from my secretary that the senator had called.

"He has been working on it. The White House sent over the appointment that runs out in December, end of the term, and an appointment in December for the next term. Republicans here are going to object to any appointment going beyond the current term. If Carter gets back in, it would be extended. Republicans, if Reagan gets in, may want to nominate someone else."

At least this was an answer. Unfortunately, it was looking less and less like Carter would win re-election. The country had grown weary of his talk about national "malaise," and his presidential weakness was best symbolized by the more than 400-day stalemate over the American hostages held in Iran.

In November, the Democrat's worst fears were realized. Reagan delivered a crushing blow on Election Day, beating Carter by one of the most lopsided margins in U.S. presidential history. And down the ticket, Regan helped sweep Republicans into power in the Senate.

On the last day of the year, the newspapers made it official that my nomination had been jettisoned:

> *Ronald Reagan's election as the next president and the shift of Senate control from Democratic to Republican hands have combined to deprive Lorain attorney E.G. Koury of a high federal job that had been tantalizingly within his grasp.*

My illusions of political grandeur were shattered. I knew, of course, that it would have helped my career, but I had also taken part in national politics for idealistic purposes. Unfortunately, the more I learned about how political appointments, prestige and fame could be gained in exchange for money running in the millions, the more disillusioned I became. Finally, I decided to get out of politics once and for all. I had been idealistic and hopeful for change, but came to understand that at its root, politics was all about money. Today this is truer than ever. The 2010 Citizens United Supreme Court decision allows corporations, labor unions and individuals to spend millions on candidates and not have to account for it under the banner of "Freedom of speech." It's a horrendous decision with far-reaching impact. But back then, things were still happening—albeit on the smaller scale. I figured I couldn't raise millions, so there was no place for me in politics. Adding fuel to the fire was an incident when I saw Clark Clifford, adviser to President Carter, and Pamela Churchill Harriman, a legendary fundraiser for the Dems at the White House. As the New York Times said, she could never put to rest the legend of the captivating woman who snared some of the world's richest and most attractive men on two continents—marrying three of them.

Seeing her and knowing that big money bought choice positions, like an ambassadorship, ignited my distaste for politics so much that I vowed to leave it. No longer was there room for my idealism in politics. As a result, I returned to Ohio with the intent of never becoming involved again.

For eight years I remained steadfast in my resolution to stay out of politics, despite two presidential candidates, Michael Dukakis and Al Gore, both Democrats vying for the 2008 nomination, wooing me for support.

Gore particularly was aggressive. His campaign assistant sought me out in Cleveland at a political meeting I had attended to hear the candidates speak. When we met he said Gore wanted to speak privately with me. I agreed. Even if I was out of politics, it wouldn't hurt to meet with a potential presidential candidate. Gore asked for my support: Could I help him deliver Ohio? I graciously refused.

A week later, he called me at my office. I was flattered. Gore invited me and Lila to join him as his guest at a $5,000 a ticket fundraiser at the Grand Ole Opry in Nashville, Tennessee. Johnny Cash was performing. Again, I politely declined.

Gore gave up after that, but it wasn't the end of candidates' pleas for my support. A few years later, Joel Hyatt was running for U.S. senator to replace his father-in-law Sen. Howard Metzenbaum. We ran into each other at a baseball game and Joel implored me to support him. But again, I politely refused. I wanted no part of politics anymore. Special interest groups were running things, and their ever-growing ability to donate cash—in the millions—turned the election process into a farce. In hindsight, my support probably would have earned me a piece of a business venture Gore and Hyatt were part of—the Newsworld International cable TV venture, which later sold to the Al Jazeera Media Network, bringing them a tidy profit.

My father probably would have berated me for bucking the world of power and politics. But I was in the process of transitioning away from that world, and heading toward a new one. And its genesis would arrive in a dramatic conversion.

Leo's Lesson Learned:
When you have integrity, you can be one of the finest people in the world.

CHAPTER 15

Redemption

After Carter's defeat, my Washington spotlight quietly faded away and I settled down to a quieter life. One day I noticed an evangelical meeting scheduled at Cleveland Municipal Stadium. The media reported that 65,000 people were expected to turn out to hear the Rev. Billy Graham.

"I wonder why so many people go to him?" I mused to myself that morning. I was still down in the dumps about a lot of things in my life and told Lila I wanted to go to the event.

Lila was puzzled. "Why do you want to go, Leo?"

"I don't have to have a reason," I explained. "I just want to know why so many people go there."

"You don't have to go," she said.

"I'm not asking for permission. I want to go."

So we went.

I'll never forget the experience. Once we arrived I looked around and said to myself, "What am I doing here?"

In that moment I knew why I didn't want to go to any of these things. They were filled with hypocrites. I knew I was a sinner, but I didn't want those hypocrites judging me. But then I heard Billy Graham's first words, and everything became crystal clear: "I, Billy Graham, am a sinner. All of us are sinners. The only person who did not sin, Jesus Christ, died on the cross. He died and His blood was for our sins. If you confess with your mouth and believe in your heart that He died for our sins, you will be saved, and the Holy Spirit will come to you. You will be born again."

I turned to Lila. "How can you be born again?"

Graham said it was the Holy Spirit. His words were so intense. I listened to everything he said, and was one of the first people to approach when Graham asked the crowd to come down. I felt different afterward, which was when my wife's friend, Jeanette Kanaan, ushered me over to that TV reporter for the interview.

The Billy Graham Crusade—and my public affirmation to Christianity—didn't turn my life into a movie script. I didn't hear heavenly bells ring, nor did I feel compelled to drop everything to go and make disciples of all nations. Instead, for several months afterward, things went along pretty much the same as they had been before the event. But beneath the surface of my complacency, powerful spiritual forces had indeed been unleashed. It was about two months after the Crusade when I gave an interview to The (Lorain) Morning Journal about my new spiritual leanings. Ironically, this was the newspaper that gave my father and me such hard criticism over the years.

"I didn't want to do this interview because it's personal to me," I said to the reporter. "I don't want it to be magnified. But if it can help one person to seek answers and change, then I'll be grateful."

My acceptance of the Lord served as a blanket invitation for Christian friends and family members to begin pounding away with renewed vigor at my now-waning spiritual resistance. Jeanette, for one, was especially insistent in her encouragement that I join a Bible study group. She also gave me the phone number of a Christian counselor—a person who I could call at any hour for encouragement and guidance along my path.

But I didn't call. And I didn't join the Bible study group. In fact, I didn't do much of anything. I stubbornly refused to plunge into the Scriptures. I didn't know much about this new faith I had recently accepted. I only knew what hit me on a visceral level: The vague appreciation that God had somehow saved my life would ensure that it would never again be quite the same for me. Wasn't that enough for now? So I avoided all the loving invitations to anchor my new faith in the recorded Word of God. I continued to swat away invitations to join Bible studies like they were pesky flies.

"I don't need it," I said, insistent as always on going my own way.

Little did I know that Christ was about to overturn my life like the way He upended Saul of Tarsus on the road to Damascus for having it his way too long.

Leo's Lesson Learned:
Get yourself in gear. Face your challenge.

CHAPTER 16
Redemption, Part II

E ventually, I would come to learn that my resistant attitude wasn't so unusual. Many new Christians feel embarrassed by their ignorance of Biblical teaching, and they often feel intimidated to put that lack of knowledge on display for others. It's why they often recoil at the thought of joining a Bible study group, which is their only real hope of grounding their new faith in something solid—the Lord's Word.

Our home arrangements changed along with me. After nearly 70 years living in Lorain, I never thought I would leave. I loved being a small-town lawyer; it gave me all the identity I ever needed. At the same time, it was the town in which I had learned that I could do anything I really wanted to do. You might say it was the source of both my roots and wings. Before my mother's death, in 1989, I never would have entertained the thought of leaving. I had silently pledged to take care of her for the rest of her life, and that meant checking in on her almost daily for all those years. But with her death and my new life as a Christian, the slates were wiped clean. Anything was possible—and that included moving from my hometown.

Increasingly, I was feeling as though God had a plan for my family, of a new life in a new place. In March 1995, I walked away from the lucrative law practice I had with 10 other lawyers in downtown Lorain. Lila and I bought a house in Westlake, Ohio, a vibrant and growing suburb west of Cleveland.

It was God's doing that coaxed me to make the move. It was my "Damascus Road experience," an extension of my Billy Graham Crusade encounter. The Bible tells us that sometime after Jesus had died and ascended into Heaven, He spoke to Saul while he was traveling to Damascus to persecute with a fury the Christian followers there. A blinding light knocked Saul to the ground. He was struck blind for three days.

Jesus made it very clear to Saul that he had gone his own way for long enough. Now Saul was to become an instrument in the hands of the Master. He took the name of Paul and became Jesus' greatest ambassador.

While this was an instantaneous experience for Paul, to other people the conversion is more of a gradual understanding of the truth of the Gospel. My experience was a bit of both, and both have several points in common. First, salvation is of the Lord, by His will, according to His plan and purpose.

Second, Saul and all others who are redeemed by Christ respond with, "What do you want me to do?" When we have that encounter with God and He truly touches our hearts, we can only say, "Lord, may your will be done; use me to do it."

So I thought it best to leave my law office without much off any explanation, hoping to not get emotional and change my mind.

At an appropriate time on a Friday, I told my associate Pat Riley, "I'll see you. I'm leaving." He said, "We'll see you Monday." I said, "No, I'm leaving." I didn't sit down and discuss it with them. That was the impact of Billy Graham. I walked out on all the hard work and years I spent building up a practice and establishing my credibility. I had the faith through Jesus Christ to leave.

I told Pat I had taken care of the outstanding cases and described what to do with payments that came in. I assured him not to worry. I felt a whole new kind of peace with a different way of life.

To help embrace that different way of life, I realized now was the opportunity to study God's word. Lila and I attended a small Bible study group at Joe and Jeanette Kanaan's home. It was us and a half dozen of our friends. Before long, this small group grew to 50 to 60 people. The Kanaans had to clear out their furniture to accommodate everyone. Another family friend, John Murtha, was the group's Bible teacher. John would become one of the most significant influences on my life from this moment forward.

The Bible study group became my rock—it made me a stronger person with greater faith. Eventually, the group became too big for the Kanaan's home, so we moved the study to our house and held it every Monday evening.

Before coming to Northeast Ohio, John served as a missionary in Thailand with his wife, Marie, and their four children. He previously had served there as a soldier during the Vietnam War. After his discharge from the armed services, John became active in teaching and preparing missionaries for overseas service as well as leading small groups. His involvement in my life was instrumental in my change— and my future.

For the next 11 years, my wife Lila opened our house for Bible study. Over the years it became something of a family affair as our children joined in. Today, my relationship with my children is something special, an affirmation of love. Beyond our love for the Bible and God's word, we take vacations together and do so many things as a family that it is a much different relationship than my father had with my mother, my siblings and me. For us, it's all about the relationship and where I am putting my focus. It's amazing how incredible life becomes when you are grounded and have your priorities in order.

Meanwhile, as word got around about my new spiritual status, I began to receive more solicitations for donations to Christian causes than I could handle. I pledged myself to the Fellowship of Christian Athletes, my church and a handful of other charities. I was still beginning to feel overwhelmed by all the other good causes—campus crusades, prison ministries and the like—that were coming at me from every direction. Finally recognizing that I was overwhelmed, I asked my friend, the retired banker and pillar of the local Christian community, Gordon Heffern, for some advice. Wasn't there a way to cut through all the charitable requests? Wasn't there one good vehicle for giving to worthy Christian causes?

But even as I posed the question, the beginnings of an answer were taking shape. I thought about the Dr. Alfred J. Loser Memorial Scholarship Fund I had helped create earlier and how one modest initial pot of money, prudently invested and wisely stewarded, had helped hundreds of Lorain students attend college over many years. When we began that fund, I didn't know anything about investing, hadn't a clue about how to choose an investment manager to oversee the funds. But God somehow led me to *Money* magazine and a feature story on just the right money manager. And again, like Jimmy Carter, he was a quiet Christian man of high moral character. And so the idea began to percolate: Why not establish a similar fund to support Christian causes?

We soon did. With my young friend Brian Morgan, a bank trust officer, we incorporated the new nonprofit foundation. The group eventually settled on an appropriate name for our fledgling foundation: In His Steps. Though my involvement was only during its early days, it's encouraging to have followed its growth over the years. After its establishment, the IHS Foundation joined the growing ranks of local Christian community foundations, which today are now sprouting up like crabgrass across the country. The leadership of IHS was setting no small goals. After meeting with the head of the venerable Cleveland Foundation, which in its more than 80 years of existence has amassed more than $1 billion, Heffern emerged with the vision that IHS would similarly top the $1 billion mark one day. The foundation got a good start. After just a year in existence, it had made excellent progress to reach that lofty goal, attracting a couple of million dollars in donations with several million more in commitments. Today, there is more than $25 million in the IHS Foundation.

While I moved out of Lorain to retire, I became fortunate to continue representing more Ohio attorney generals as special counsel— I've served 10 in all, including current Attorney General Mike DeWine—in my association with five other lawyers. All these people revived my practice. In fact, my practice was growing! In doing so, I learned from my associates how to share, how to be a Christian and how to give back to people. That wasn't my original intention, which was to retire. But now, I felt a new focus on philanthropy.

It's amazing to think about all the lessons I've learned in my life so far. One of the most important is that there is nothing to life but love. My grandfather embedded that in me. Subconsciously, I had it in my heart but I would never express it for fear of rejection, for fear of being hurt, or the fear of being seen as weak.

But now, because I have God, whom shall I fear? Everything I do is for His glory and the manifestation of His presence.

Leo's Lesson Learned:
Things happen in life for a reason. Learn how to embrace change.

CHAPTER 17

Amazing Grace

My experience at the Billy Graham Crusade was my first step toward a Christian awakening. That was more than 20 years ago. In those two decades I have learned the importance of reading the Bible and having support through fellowship. We are vessels, the Bible says. But we are imperfect, and the Holy Spirit leaks out from our vessel-selves. We are refilled by reading the Bible and sharing in fellowship the stories of our journeys. And mine has been a long and interesting journey—filled with twists and turns.

Fellowship is an important part of the journey because it constantly keeps you thinking about what's important in your life. And over my life, what's been considered important has evolved.

My father wanted me to be successful yet compassionate. This was his goal all along, part of every calculated action he took while raising me. I recall when I was a young man and he said, "Son, you're going to become a lawyer. But always remember this: Treat the poor just like you treat the wealthy. Do your job for the poor and the wealthy without thought of money or being paid. If you do your job for the people and you're doing it as a professional, the money will come."

I didn't really understand it at the time, but followed his advice. And for the first 10 years of my career, I spent my time working hard and trying to build a respectable name for myself through my actions. That meant treating people well while I learned everything there was to learn about practicing law.

God's grace is bountiful with unearned blessings, and I'm amazed at the blessings I've received. If you ask me to summarize my life so far, it goes something like this: Leo Koury is basically a good guy—a sinner saved by God's grace. He's not an intellect and not the best lawyer. But one of his strengths is that he strives to live his life in the service of others.

Remember what Gen. George Marshall said: "Constant honesty creates instant credibility." I hope that so far, I've lived up to those words.

Before my transformation I had love, but no understanding of where it came from. I knew it was important to treat others with respect and loyalty, but never recognized why. You can love someone and not be loyal to them—think about the man who loves his wife but cheats on her. I did many sinful things because we are all born sinful, but I never intentionally tried to hurt anyone. Those who forgave me taught me the love of Christ—especially my wife, Lila. I was hardly ever home for the kids because I was working around the clock to earn a living. And Lila knew whenever I did something wrong, but never judged or criticized me. Isn't that the greatest forgiveness one can give?

Make no mistake about it, every day is a challenge. I don't walk around with a halo above my head. Some days, I might get mad talking on the telephone when I know I shouldn't. Other days, I might feel rejected but quickly recognize that's my pride getting in the way. I am not a perfect man. I know this. But I try every day to humbly serve the Lord.

God taught me numerous lessons. One of my favorite is Luke 12:48, which says "To whom much is given, much will be required." It's a reason why I try to be involved in philanthropic causes. Another verse I love is Romans 8:31, which states "If God be for us, who can be against us?" But I don't just sit around and quote the Bible. Instead, I try to live the messages and become a better person.

I used to be full of myself and let my ego run the show. But today, I recognize that He was always around me, guiding me, helping me shape the decisions I've made in my life and providing the blessings of success for me and my family. God did this for me—that I know. And, I'm a much more humble man because of it.

Every morning, Lila and I read the Bible and say a prayer. After the prayer we read an excerpt from a daily devotional magazine and then we read a lesson from Billy Graham. Finally, before I leave the house I read from one of the many books I have that offer Christian messages. I need all of this every day—and I need the fellowship. It is a constant reminder that nothing in this world is about me, and that by focusing on others I can enjoy the world that much more.

This outlook on life has made it much easier not to judge people. It's also allowed me to try to focus every conversation I have throughout the day on others instead of me. It's not easy, but I try to listen and hear other people's problems or needs, and then identify ways I might be able to help. My father instilled in me a desire to see the world through other people's eyes—to find ways to help them without thinking about what's in it for me.

Before my awakening, I had a big chip on my shoulder. I was a bootlegger's son and was determined to prove that not only wasn't my father a criminal but instead a man of integrity and loyalty. Today, that chip is gone. Now I wear my legacy—and my father's name, which I gave to my eldest son—as a badge of honor.

So what would my father think of me now? He told me to be compassionate to others. He told me to be tough. He told me to be a man. Would he be happy with the man I've become?

Yes, I believe he would.

As I reflect back on the life I've lived so far, I've come to recognize a lot about myself. For example, the reason I was never close to Christianity or fellowship was that I knew I was a sinner and didn't want to be judged. This changed in 1994 when I attended the Billy Graham Crusade. Billy Graham showed me how to open my arms and heart. Today, my love is more easily expressed because I no longer fear rejection. When you have the Lord, there is no reason to fear.

Just as important, my faith has taught me not to judge people. I used to do that a lot—to the point where I often wanted to get even with those whom I believed had wronged me. Author Wayne Dyer described the idea of forgiving others well: "Forgiveness means that you fill yourself with love and you radiate that love outward and refuse to hang onto the venom or hatred that was engendered by the behaviors that caused the wounds."

Twenty years ago, I decided to begin forgiving people from my past. It was difficult at first. To be honest, I needed help from my son, Fred, who sat me down and insisted I learn how to forgive.

Once I forgave the first person, it became easier and soon there was a flood. As a result, all the bitterness in my life that had stained my soul melted away. Before becoming a Christian I didn't understand that transgressions were something to be forgiven. But that has now become crystal clear.

It was the hardest to forgive people whom I felt were hypocrites—those who called me a "bootlegger's son" yet had their own checkered pasts. Jesus says to forgive sinners "seventy times seven." Often, I've wondered what that means. I've come to believe that means forgive from your heart, so I look for ways to go beyond saying the words "I forgive you" and speak louder through my actions.

For example, when I saw one of my former nemeses at a reception sitting alone I went up to him, kissed him on the top of his head and asked, "How are you feeling?

"Just hanging in there," he replied.

"If you ever get to Cleveland, please call me," I said. "I will take you to lunch."

That was my simple act of forgiveness—inviting him into my life.

There is little doubt that God has blessed me with this new Christian life. And because of that I try to set an example by not lecturing or judging—whether they are sinner or not. Christ ministered to sinners, the infirmed and others, and because of His teaching I can share that inclusiveness.

Not long ago I traveled to the Billy Graham Library in Charlotte, North Carolina. We were met and escorted to the nearby Billy Graham Evangelistic Association headquarters by Wayne Atcheson, historian, and Tom Phillips, executive director, at the Billy Graham Library. They took us into Billy Graham's office, where I received a birthday card and a bronze copy of the gold medallion of Billy and Ruth Graham presented to them by Congress. This was a replica of the Congressional Gold Medal originally given to George Washington.

The visit opened my eyes to what was the most hopeful word in history: Salvation.

Graham explains salvation in his book, "Reason for My Hope: Salvation." He says that "we receive salvation from our selfish and self-destructive selves; the messes we get ourselves into; the sin that has haunted humanity from the beginning of time; the evil that pulls us down every day; the cultural deceits that blind us to God's saving message; and from the hell so many don't believe in."

All of this moved me. I felt like I had been living in a vacuum all my life, not knowing what salvation was really all about. But I came to understand that life was really about having a relationship with God through Jesus Christ and sharing that love with others—and that, in my opinion, is a successful life!

It's no coincidence that I named my son Fred to honor my father. It helps me remember him and everything he means to me.

So how would I sum up my life? Simple. I have found peace and contentment, and through my relationship with God have come to honor my father. Not too bad for a so-called bootlegger's son.

Leo's Lesson Learned:
What I learned is that life is not all about me,
but rather knowing God and sharing his love with others.

LEO'S 12 TIPS FOR A BETTER LIFE

1. Get right with God to become a practicing Christian.

2. Tell your loved ones you love them regularly.

3. Marry someone who brings out the best in you.

4. Affirm to yourself that each day is a blessing.

5. Be honest. "Constant honesty creates instant credibility."
   —George Marshall.

6. Give your resources to others less fortunate than you.

7. Hard work tempers your personality and teaches you values.

8. Believe in yourself, but be humble.

9. Learn from a mentor, in your business and your spiritual lives.

10. Become a selfless person; have humility; think of others.

11. Education is of paramount importance. Read, and read well.

12. Surround yourself with people better than yourself, and avoid those not motivated to improve themselves.

ABOUT THE AUTHOR

E.G. "Leo" Koury grew up in the shadow of a mammoth steel mill in Lorain, Ohio, that not only defined its hardscrabble neighborhood, but supplied the customers for his family's Mill Tavern—Leo's prep school in life. He never appreciated his bootlegger father's strict discipline and criticism at the time and how it placed a chip on his shoulder, but it motivated him to become a lawyer. After military service, however, he found himself an unemployed attorney until getting a break from the Democratic Party chairman that set him on a path to a successful career in law, business and politics.

Years later when Leo experienced God's amazing grace at a Billy Graham Crusade, it all came full circle—Leo realized who his father was, how to honor him and then how his life turned around with his heavenly Father, to commit his life to Christ. Leo's career as a successful lawyer was punctuated by events he later realized were God at work, such as when he helped Jimmy Carter garner precious votes to grasp the presidency and the launch of many philanthropic efforts to give back to others.

He and his wife Lila are the parents of four children and live near Cleveland, Ohio.